AF553348

© 2014

ISBN: 978-81-7141-666-0

© Authors

Child Labour and Agriculture

Published by:

DISCOVERY PUBLISHING HOUSE PVT. LTD.
4383/4B, Ansari Road, Darya Ganj
New Delhi-110 002 (India)
Phone: +91-11-23279245, 43596064-65
Fax: +91-11-23253475
E-mail: discoverypublishinghouse@gmail.com
sales@discoverypublishinggroup.com
web: www.discoverypublishinggroup.com

Printed at:
Infinity Imaging Systems
Delhi

Preface

Although the internationally recommended minimum age for work is 15 years and the number of child workers under the age of 10 is far from negligible, almost all the data available on child labour concerns the 10-to-14 age group.

Traditionally, the proportion of working children has been much higher in rural than in urban areas—nine out of ten are engaged in agricultural or related activities. In the towns and cities of India where child labour has increased steadily as a result of the rapid urbanization of recent years, working children are found mainly in trade and services and to a lesser extent in the manufacturing section.

Available statistics suggest that more boys than girls work. It should be borne in mind, however, that the number of working girls in often under estimated by statistical surveys, as they usually do not take into account full-time housework performed by many children, the vast majority of whom are girls, in order to enable their parents to go to work.

Girls, moreover, tend to work longer hours, on average, than do boys. This is especially true for the many girls employed as domestic workers, a type of employment in which hours of work are typically extremely long. This is also the case of girls employed in other types of jobs who, in addition to their professional activity, must help with the housework in their parents' home.

One of the factors affecting the supply of child labour is the high cost, in real terms, of obtaining an education. Many children work to cover the costs of school expenses. But, many schools serving the poor are of such abysmal quality or chances of upward mobility for graduates are so slim, that the expected return is not equal to the sacrifice made.... While it is true that many children drop out of school because they have to work, it is equally true that many become so discouraged by school that they prefer to work.

In manufacturing industries, children are most likely to be employed when their labour is less expensive or less troublesome than that of adults, when other labour is scarce, and when they are considered irreplaceable by reason of their size or perceived dexterity.

Many working children face significant threats to their health and safety. The majority are involved in farming and are routinely exposed to harsh climate, sharpened tools, heavy loads as well, increasingly, as to toxic chemicals and motorized equipment. Others, particularly girls working as domestic servants away from their homes, are frequent victims of physical, mental and sexual abuses which can have devastating consequences on their health.

Dr. M. Lakshmi Narasaiah

Contents

1

Child Labour—Targeting the Intolerable

We all know that child labour is one of the faces of poverty and that many efforts over many years will be required to eliminate it completely. But, there are some forms of child labour today which are intolerable by any standard. These deserve to be identified, exposed are eradicated without further delay.

The problem of child labour is so enormous and the need for action is urgent, choices must be made about where to concentrate available human and material resources. The most humane strategy must therefore be to focus scarce resources first on the most intolerable forms of child labour such as slavery, debt bondage child prostitution, work in hazardous occupations and industries, and the very young, especially girls.

In addition, a comparative study carried out over a period of 17 years in India on both children who attend school and children who instead work in agriculture, industry or the service sector showed that working children grow up shorter and weigh less than school children.

In Bombay, the health of children working in hotels, restaurants, construction and elsewhere was found to be considerably inferior to that of a control group of non working school children. Working children exhibited symptoms of constant muscular, chest and abdominal pain, headaches, dizziness, respiratory, infections, diarrhoea and worm infection.

Sexual Differences

Girls more often work in domestic labour, boys work in construction, fields and factories, leading to sexual differences in exposure to hazards. Girls, because of their employment in households, work longer hours than boys each day. This is one important reason why girls receive less schooling than boys. Girls are also more vulnerable than boys to sexual abuse and its consequences, such as social rejection, psychological trauma and unwanted motherhood. Boys, on the other hand, tend to suffer more injuries resulting from carrying weights too heavy for their age and stage of physical development. There are unsafe and abusive working situations for children. Some examples of these include:

- ***Slavery and Forced Child Labour:*** Of all working children, those bound in slavery and forced child labour are the most imperiled. Children are still being sold outright for a sum of money. At other times, landlords buy child workers from their tenants, or labour 'contractors' pay rural families in advance in order to take their children away to work in carpet-weaving, glass manufacturing or prostitution.
- ***Prostitution and Trafficking of Children:*** The commercial sexual exploitation of children is on the rise, even though the subject has in recent years become an issue of global concern. Children are increasingly being bought and sold across national borders by organised networks.
- *Agriculture:* Children work in agriculture throughout the world and often face hazards through exposure to biological and chemical agents. Children can be found mixing, loading and applying pesticides, fertilizers or herbicides, some of which are highly toxic and potentially carcinogenic. Pesticide exposure poses a

considerably higher risk to children than to adults, and has been linked to an increased risk of cancer, neuropathy, neuro-behavioural effects and immune system abnormalities.

Mortality among child farm workers from pesticide poisoning is greater than from a combination of childhood diseases such as malaria, tetanus, diphtheria, polio and whooping cough. The operation of farm machinery by children also leads to many accidents which kill and maim.

- *Mining:* Child labour is used in small-scale mines in many countries. Child miners work long hours without adequate protective equipment, clothing or training. They are also exposed to high humidity levels and extreme temperatures.

  Mining hazards include exposure to harmful dusts, gases and fumes that cause respiratory diseases that can develop into silicosis, pulmonary fibrosis, asbestosis and emphysema after some years of exposure. Child miners also suffer from physical strain, fatigue and musculoskeletal disorders, as well as serious injuries from falling objects. Children working in gold mines and endangered by mercury poisoning.

- *Ceramics and glass factory work:* Child labour in these industries is common. Children often must carry molten loads of glass dragged from tank furnaces at a temperature of 1500-1800 degrees Centigrade. They also work lon[illegible]rs in rooms with poor lighting and little or no vent[illegible]on. The temperature inside these factories, some of which operate only at night, ranges from 40 to 45 degrees Centigrade. Floors are covered with broken glass and in many cases electric wires are exposed. The noise level from glass-pressing machines can be as high as 100 decibels or more, causing hearing impairment.

  The main hazards in this industry are exposure to high temperatures leading to heat stress, cataracts, burns and lacerations; injuries from broken glass and flying glass particles; hearing impairment from noise; eye injuries and eye strain from poor lighting; and exposure to silica dust, lead and toxic fumes such as carbon monoxide and sulphur dioxide.

- ***Matches and fireworks industry:*** Match production normally takes place in small cottage units or in small-scale village factories where the risk of fire and explosion is present at all times. Children as young as three are reported to work in match factories in unventilated rooms where they are exposed to dust, fumes, vapours and airborne concentrations of hazardous substances—asbestos, potassium chlorate, antimony trisulphide, amorphous red phosphorous mixed with sand or powdered glass and tetraphosphorous trisulphide. Intoxication and dermatitis from these substances are frequent.

- ***Deep-sea fishing:*** In many Asian countries, children work in muro-ami fishing, which involves deep-sea diving without the use of protective equipment. The children beat on coral reefs to scare the fish into nets. Each fishing ship employs up to 300 boys between ages 10 and 15 recruited from poor neighbourhoods. Divers reset the nets several times a day, so that the children are often in the water for up to 12 hours. Dozens of children are killed or injured each year from drowning or from decompression sickness or fatal accidents from exposure to high atmospheric pressure. Predatory fish such as sharks, barracudas, needle-fish and poisonous sea snakes also attack the children.

- ***Child domestic workers:*** Child domestic service is a widespread practice in many developing countries, with employers in cities often recruiting children from rural villages through family, friends and contacts. Violence and sexual abuse are among the most serious and frightening hazards facing children at work, specially those in domestic service. Such abuse leads to permanent psychological and emotional damage.

- ***Construction:*** Children undertaking heavy work, carrying massive loads and maintaining awkward body positions for a long time can develop deformation of the spinal column. Sometimes, the pelvis can also be deformed because of excessive stress being placed on the bones before the epiphysis has fused. Children working in construction and other fields are exposed to other toxic and carcinogenic substances, including asbestos, one of the best known of human carcinogens.

One reason why modern societies and governments have not been more active in curbing the most harmful forms of child labour is that working children are often not readily visible. It is a matter of 'out of sight' 'out of mind'.

2

Stop Child Labour

Although the internationally recommended minimum age for work is 15 years and the number of child workers under the age of 10 is far from negligible, almost all the data available on child labour concerns the 10-to-14 age group.

Traditionally, the proportion of working children has been much higher in rural than in urban areas—nine out of ten are engaged in agricultural or related activities. In the towns and cities of India where child labour has increased steadily as a result of the rapid urbanisation of recent years, working children are found mainly in trade and services and to a lesser extent in the manufacturing section.

Available statistics suggest that more boys than girls work. It should be borne in mind, however, that the number of working girls is often under estimated by statistical surveys, as they usually do not take into account full-time housework performed by many children, the vast majority of whom are girls, in order to enable their parents to go to work.

Girls, moreover, tend to work longer hours, on average, than do boys. This is especially true for the many girls employed as domestic workers, a type of employment in which hours of work are typically extremely long. This is also the case of girls employed in other types of jobs who, in addition to their professional activity, must help with the housework in their parents' home.

One of the factors affecting the supply of child labour is the high cost, in real terms, of obtaining an education. Many children work to cover the costs of school expenses. But, many schools serving the poor are of such abysmal quality or chances of upward mobility for graduates are so slim, that the expected return is not equal to the sacrifice made.... While it is true that many children drop out of school because they have to work, it is equally true that many become so discouraged by school that they prefer to work.

In manufacturing industries, children are most likely to be employed when their labour is less expensive or less troublesome than that of adults, when other labour is scarce, and when they are considered irreplaceable by reason of their size or perceived dexterity.

Many working children face significant threats to their health and safety. The majority are involved in farming and are routinely exposed to harsh climate, sharpened tools, heavy loads as well, increasingly, as to toxic chemicals and motorized equipment. Others, particularly girls working as domestic servants away from their homes, are frequent victims of physical, mental and sexual abuses which can have devastating consequences on their health.

Prostitution is another type of activity in which children, especially girls, are increasingly found. The AIDS epidemic is a contributing factor to this trend, as adults see the use of children for sexual purposes as the best means of preventing infection. The laissez-faire attitude of the authorities incharge of national and international tourism is also largely responsible for the current situation.

Another extremely serious problem is child slavery in India. A large number of child slaves are to be found in agriculture, domestic help, the sex industry, the carpet and textile industries, quarrying and brickmaking. Child slavery predominates mainly where there are social systems based on the exploitation of poverty, such as debt bondage, when the motivation is the debt incurred by a family to meet a social of religious obligation or simply to acquire the means of survival.

There is a growing body of opinion that national and international efforts need to be more sharply focused on the most abusive and hazardous forms of child labour, granting them first concern and priority. Perhaps the most telling social argument against child labour is that its effects are highly discriminatory, adding to the burden and disadvantage of individuals and groups already among the socially excluded while benefiting those who are privileged. For that reason, child labour is inconsistent with democracy and social justice.

Action Required at the National Level

In the majority of states of India where child labour is common, the action taken until now to combat it has in no way been proportional to the extent and gravity of the problem. Many state governments have left it to economic growth and legislation alone to provide the solution. Experience has shown however that, unless specific measures are taken, growth in itself rarely benefits the very poor and that legislation means little where it is not vigorously enforced.

The problem of child labour will not be solved overnight. It is one of the many facets of poverty and underdevelopment. Resources available to reduce its extent and damaging effects are by definition scarcest in India that need them the most. Priorities must therefore be set.

No Effective Programmes Without Hard Information

Research: Almost everywhere, hard information is lacking on how many children are working, what they are doing, where and in what conditions. Without such data, it is virtually impossible to develop effective policies and programmes. Establishing, in some cases improving, data collection systems on child labour is an essential first step.

Raising Awareness: A common attitude toward child labour in India is to accept it as an unavoidable consequence of poverty. Given the low quality and implied costs of the education services available to the poor, many parents, having themselves worked as children, tend to consider an early entry into the labour market, rather than schooling, as the best way to equip their children with skills useful for their future as adults.

Another difficulty is inherent in the fact that children working in rural areas, in urban informal sector workshops or as domestic servants in private households are not readily visible. An effective effort to protect children from work place hazards or abuses must therefore begin by making the invisible visible. Experience clearly shows that significant public pressure is required to make progress on the child labour issue politically possible. As long as the general public, and in particular the middle and higher classes, consider that child labour is part of the harsh reality that makes good economic sense, the conditions for change will not be met.

The Government of India has restricted its role to enacting legislation, but has been passive in its enforcement. Most initiatives against child labour have traditionally come from Non-Government Organisations. In spite of their dedication however, their resources cannot be equal to the magnitude of the task. All levels of society need to do their share.

Some types of action can be provided only by the central government: child labour legislation and attendant enforcement mechanisms, the setting of public policy priorities and a publicly-funded system of basic education that offers quality schooling for all, including the children of the poorest families.

Trade Unions Bring Abuses to Light

Trade unions, are the logical leaders for bringing child labour abuses to light. They are ideally placed to document concrete cases of abusive child labour and to monitor the effectiveness of legal instruments and the performance of the labour inspectorate in the child labour field.

Employers and their organisations also have good reasons to be interested in the issue. Besides obvious humanitarian and social reasons, combating child labour makes perfect sense on economic and business grounds. Emotionally or physically damaged children have little chance of becoming productive adults.

NGOs' Strength is with Children Already Working

Like trade unions, NGOs can help to discover and publicise specific cases of abusive child labour. They are, in addition especially good at devising and implementing action programmes on behalf of children already in the labour market. Close to the children, they generally enjoy the trust of the local communities concerned and are well placed to appeal to their hearts and resources.

The participation of other segments of civil society—the media, universities, parliamentarians, teachers and educators—should be enlisted in the fight against child labour. All are valuable allies and can cooperate in complementary ways.

Establishing the Required Institutional Capacity: To formulate and execute a national plan of action against child labour, institutional mechanisms must be established or strengthened within the governmental apparatus. These can then be entrusted with the responsibility for setting priorities, coordinating the activities of the various ministries concerned, promoting private sector participation and for launching and supporting pilot schemes to find new ways of preventing child labour and of rehabilitating those who have been rescued from it.

Improving Legislation and Enforcement Measures: In India legislation exempts from coverage precisely the kinds of work in which children are most engaged (agriculture, family undertakings, small workshops, domestic service). A necessary first step to expanding protection under the law is to ensure that the main places where children work and the worst forms of child labour are encompassed by national legislation.

Improving Schooling for the Poor: The single most effective way to stem the flow of school-age children into abusive forms of employment or work is to extend and improve schooling so that it will attract and retain them. Recent trends however leave little room for optimism in that regard. In the eighties and early nineties resources devoted to education have dwindled steadily in India. The poor situation of the economy and the effects of structural adjustment policies were the reasons generally given for this decline.

Using Economic Incentives: As poor families need the income deriving from the employment of their children, it has often been considered appropriate to provide cash or in-kind payments as replacement.

Lively International Debate Over Negative Incentives: The advisability of using negative economic incentives has been the subject of much recent public debate. In Europe several department stores have decided not to sell products such as carpets unless they are certified to be made without child labour. Such movements by consumers and manufacturers alike have been accompanied by powerful efforts on the legislative and trade fronts as demonstrated by the hot debate on the incorporation of a social clause into international trade agreements. The United States has introduced conditionality into its generalised system of preferences, as has the European Union, to promote, among others, better labour standards and thereby discourage the use of child labour. A bill aiming at banning the import into the United States of goods produced by children (the Harkin Bill), has generated concern among employers and governments in countries heavily dependent on the United States for their exports.

There is no doubt that initiatives of this kind have helped significantly to raise public awareness about child labour. However, they have also had unintended consequences. The mere threat led employers of various industries to abruptly dismiss tens of thousands of children, the end result was that.

3

Child Labour in Weaving Industry

Approximately 1,30,000 children work in India's hand-knotted carpet industry. The working conditions are often poor, involving long hours sitting in one position, breathing cotton and wool fibres, eye-strain from doing very fine work and poor lighting. In the smallest enterprises the only light often available is the natural light filtering in through an open doorway.

Children are more likely to work in larger establishments: the smallest enterprises are family operations where the father and other family members might both weave carpets and till a plot of land, whereas the larger business use almost all hired labour. In the one-loom enterprises, approximately 14 per cent of weavers are children, while the number of child labourers rises to around 33 per cent in businesses with five or more looms.

Although the proportion of child labour rises with the size of firm, the proportion does not rise as the quality of carpet increases; in fact, children are more likely to work on low-quality than on the highest-quality carpets. There is "no evidence that children dominate any particular design or quality niches". The opposite would be the case if the 'nimble fingers' argument were true.

If the 'nimble fingers' argument does not hold in the hand-knotted carpet industry, then it probably does not hold in other industries. Rejection of the 'nimble fingers' argument is reinforced by the ability of adults to master carpet-weaving skills. Many adolescents and young adults who attend government training centres go on to run their own weaving businesses, while weavers say it takes a year to become fully proficient, whether one starts as an adult or a child.

Enterprises Often Small and Impoverished

The workforce of the hand-knotted carpet industry is mired in poverty. Most weaving enterprises in the Indian hand-knotted carpet industry are small, marginal operations run by poor and illiterate men, and they have no margin to pay higher wages. Most of the employers have never attended school; then began weaving before age 14. An enterprise normally consists of a loom set up in a family's one-room cottage, with perhaps an additional loom, or looms, in an attached verandah or a shed. Male family members, including children, provide the bulk of the labour.

India's Factories Act has influenced the current structure of the carpet industry. Costly health, safety and labour regulations to which large firms are subject do not apply to cottage industries. Only a small proportion of establishment have five or more looms.

Competition Limits Retail Price Increases

While child and adult weavers have similar productivity, there is a cost advantage to hiring child labour: children earn less while apprentices than do fully-trained weavers, and their addition to the workforce depresses the going wage rate. Replacing the 22 per cent of children in the workforce would likely cause the wage bill to rise by about 5 per cent.

Given the small scale of many weaving enterprises and the fact that weaving charges make up approximately 40 per cent of the total production cost, with the loom owner receiving a fee equivalent to 10 per cent of production costs for supervision and provision of looms and premises, it is clear that the use of child labour can add greatly to the revenues and profits of looms owners.

The extra labour costs involved in eliminating child labour become much easier to absorb further down the distribution chain. Importing country wholesalers mark up the carpets around 65 per cent, while foreign retailers typically mark up the carpets by approximately 200 per cent. With sales or value-added tax, the carpets can easily cost four times as much to the consumer as the Indian export price. This means that the overall savings in production costs from the use of child labour are very small when compared to the foreign retail price.

Finding solutions which satisfy both local weavers and foreign retailers must avoid a beggar-thy-neighbour spiral. If carpet producing countries simultaneously implemented a no-child-labour strategy in their hand-knotted carpet industries, none of them would be at a competitive disadvantage.

Methods of reducing child labour such as those used in the garment industry where there is tripartite collaboration to ensure that the children are treated well and that there are educational opportunities for them until they are replaced without economic hardship to their families, is not likely to work in the hand-knotted carpet industry. Neither labelling nor inspection is likely to work here because the industry is too fragmented. It is impossible to control the thousands of cottages where one or two carpets per year are woven. We need solutions that address the general problems of poverty while developing alternative sources of both employment and education.

Child labour is not necessary in the carpet industry. Children do not possess a unique skill and there is a ready pool of surplus adult labour ready to take over from them. "People should not be fooled into thinking that child labour is necessary for the industry to survive. The irreplaceable skills, or 'nimble fingers' argument should no longer be used to justify the use of child labour in the carpet industry or any other industry."

4

Helping Your Child Learn

A one-syllable word begins the education process: 'Why'? Parents are always trying to answer that question. And that interaction between parent and child is the basis of much that children learn.

Teaching and learning are not mysteries that can happen only in school. They can also happen when parents and children do simple things together—things such as:

- Figure out whose socks are whose-sorting is a major function in maths and science.
- Cook a meal to learn science and good health.
- Tell each other a story as an important beginning for reading and writing; if the story is about the past, it's a way to interest a child in history.
- Plan a visit to a friend or relative for a personal connection with geography.
- Or play a game of hopscotch to develop counting and lifelong fitness.
- All children love their friends. So ask your child to describe his friend's appearance at the end of each school day. You can ask questions like. "What outfit

did he/she wear?" or "How did he/she do his/her hair?" This kind of routine query would encourage your child to observe his friend more minutely.

- If your child goes to school by bus, he can be asked to describe his route and point out certain landmarks namely colourful posters, traffic signals, large shops etc.

By doing things with their children, parents show that learning is fun and important—and that encourages children to study, learn, and stay in school.

Even on the discipline front, parents can help their children. Basic disciplinary principles must be tailored to each child and family. Before parents can become effective disciplinarians, they must first learn how to manage their own anger, solve problem situations and give and get support from others. Simple self-help techniques with or without professional support can help parents sharply reduce discipline problems.

Parents who are sensitive to their children's needs have more obedient children. Praise and love alone are not enough to instill good behaviour. Too much permissiveness hurts a child's efforts to develop self-control.

Behaviour problems should be reversed early. Waiting until the preteen-age years diminishes chances for success and puts children at higher risk for drug use and other problems.

Parents need to learn as many tricks of the trade as possible, including how to play with their children, communicate with them, praise and reward them and also set limits for them, as well as how to handle misbehaviour using a variety of techniques.

All that parents need to help their children is a willingness to observe and learn with them, and, to take the time to nurture their natural curiosity.

5

Children's Health and the Environment

Children today live in an environment vastly different from that of a few generations ago. Economic development, increased urbanisation and the consequences of war in many countries have added to the traditional environmental hazards, those problems associated with environmental pollution. Thus, while some traditional children's diseases such as diarrhoea, malnutrition and infectious diseases persist in many countries, environmentally-related illnesses such as asthma, respiratory illnesses due to environmental tobacco smoke (ETS), as well as mortality and morbidity due to injuries, are increasing. In childhood cancer in some countries and the potential risks of endocrine-disrupting chemicals are among the emerging health threats that need careful vigilance. Children of lower socio-economic status are likely to suffer disproportionately from all these health threats as a consequence of living in highly polluted environments, poor quality housing, lower levels of education, and of restricted access to environmental and health care services.

Children's Vulnerability

The concern for children's vulnerability to environmental health threats is based on several factors. Children receive greater exposures than adults do because they drink more water, eat more food and have higher breathing rates per unit of body weight. Because they are undergoing rapid growth and development, toxicant effects at specific times may have irreversible consequences. For example, if vital connections between nerve cells fail to form during brain development, there is high risk that the resulting neurobehavioural dysfunction will be permanent and irreversible. Also, because most children have more future years of life than adults, they have more time to develop any chronic disease that may be triggered by early environmental exposures.

Public Health Threats

Asthma, injuries, and the effects of environmental tobacco smoke (ETS) are among the most significant public health threats to children. Childhood asthma is increasingly prevalent in almost all countries. What causes asthma is not known, but several environmental factors, such as indoor air quality (particularly exposure to the house-dust mite) and ETS, have been linked with the increase in asthma. In addition, outdoor air pollutants such as particulates, sulphur dioxide and ozone can exacerbate asthma symptoms. ETS, especially smoking by the mother, is a known risk factor for asthma. ETS is also known to cause acute and chronic middle ear disease and is associated with sudden infant death syndrome (SIDS).

Potential for Prevention

The variation in asthma and injury rates and the evidence of the role of certain environmental factors underline the potential for prevention. Public policies should seek to avoid preventable childhood diseases by preventing exposures to environmental agents and considering children's characteristics and susceptibilities in the development of environmental health legislation. Promoting citizen awareness and participation in policy-making through education and access to environmental information are important elements in achieving a safe environment for children. In this context, children are not only consumers with rights, but also citizens who can play an active role towards their own protection.

International Awareness

Several international agreements have acknowledged children's vulnerabilities and have committed their signatories to protect children's health from the effects of a deteriorating environment. This year, many countries will address several of the environmental health threats to children through international and national action. It is expected that a large international collaborative initiative will result under the guidance of WHO and other international organisations.

6

Opening Markets for Agriculture

While the Uruguay Round made a good start—more was done to liberalise agricultural trade and to bring agriculture into the system than in all previous rounds combined—we have to recognise that agriculture still has a long way to go to complete its reform and to be fully integrated into the world trading system. Prior to the Uruguay Round, agricultural trading rules were not in concert with other sectors. The Uruguay Round Agreement (URAA) made good first steps toward bringing agriculture into conformity with international trade rules governing other goods, but much remains to be done.

The Uruguay Round, of course, required certain reductions in trade-distorting measures, and the implementation of those reforms has proceeded very well. Two other legacies of the Uruguay Round are very important for the new negotiations—a mandate to continue what was begun, and a structure for achieving liberalisation. The WTO's 'built-in' agenda includes agriculture. It was recognised from the outset that the first period of reform that we are still implementing was only a down payment.

In addition to the commitment to continue negotiations, the URAA—focusing on export subsidies, market access, and domestic support—established a structure on which to build. Establishing a three-pillar structure was the most time-consuming undertaking in the round. Fortunately, we do not need to reinvent that wheel. The structure of the rules provides a logical approach for the negotiations, one which most seem to agree we should keep and build on.

Export Competition

Export subsidies are an illegitimate policy instrument, a symptom of a systemic imbalance in a nation's agricultural policies, the costs of which re-borne by others. The costs of domestic policy choices should be borne by the country that chooses them, not foisted onto its trading partners by subsidising exports. The Uruguay Round made a start at eliminating agricultural export subsidies: 36 per cent reduction of budget expenditures on export subsidies and 21 per cent reduction of quantities over a six-year implementation period. With experience to show that markets adapt, we should now be able to improve the pace of export subsidy reductions and eliminate the export subsidy scourge from agricultural trade. Export subsidies are not allowed in the WTO rules for any other industry. Their use constitutes a source of trade distortion and degradation to the environment, and there is no valid reason to keep them any longer.

Market Access

The Uruguay Round progress on market access leaves much to be done. It left tariffs too high, and it did not create much new market access. The average non-agricultural tariff is now 4 per cent, while the average agricultural tariff is over 40 per cent, and tariffs on some products exceed 300 per cent. With a few exceptions, nontariff barriers were converted to tariffs, and members were required to open up at least a small minimum access—3 per cent of domestic consumption initially, growing to 5 per cent by the end of the adjustment period—under tariff-rate quotas.

The stage has been set for real reforms. Let access continue to grow and let all tariffs be reduced to negotiated maximum level by the end of the transition period. In addition, an examination of the administration of tariff-rate quotas should lead to transparent and open systems.

Many WTO members note that importers were required to change nontariff barriers to tariffs and grant access, while no reciprocal disciplines were imposed on export restraints of exporting countries. Net food importing countries should be able to expect that if they open their border to international market, those international markets will deliver supplies as reliably to importers as to the domestic markets of exporters. Willingness on the part of leading exporting members to discipline export controls will reassure 'food security' countries that expanding market access is not risky.

Domestic Support

The Aggregate Measure of Support was a success as a component of the Agreement on Agriculture and the insistence on reducing trade-distorting measures. The drive toward decoupled support ('green box') is the key. By the end of 1996, the United States had largely decoupled farm programmes so that payments to farmers were not linked to a requirement to produce. Other WTO members will also succeed in orienting their policies toward market signals. In the new round, further review and decreases in the aggregate measure of support will clearly lead to market-based agricultural trade.

A new buzzword that some countries are using to justify domestic support is 'multi functionality'. It is a buzzword for what everybody in agriculture has known for thousands of years: agriculture serves other purposes besides producing food and fiber. But the real problem with the discussion of multi-functionality is not semantic. It is the confusion between policy goals and policy instruments. If the United States appears skeptical about the implications of multi-functionality for WTO rules, the U.S. objection is not multi-functionality as a factual matter. Each country chooses social objectives for themselves. There is no inherent connection between those objectives and trade-distorting agricultural policies.

New Issues

While the Uruguay Round established effective disciplines in traditional problem areas, such disciplines have not yet been established in some new areas. As monopolies, state trading enterprises (STEs) can distort trade, and they frequently operate behind a veil of secrecy. The agricultural trading system has much to gain from WTO disciplines on STEs because they allow some countries to undercut exports based on open market transactions and restrict imports.

Biotechnology holds tremendous promise globally for food consumers, producers, and the environment. With the world's population growing by about 2 per cent annually, there are 80 million more mouths to feed each year. Some countries threaten to adopt policies regarding the importation and planting of bio-engineered crops and the labeling of products containing bio-engineered foods that are not based on scientifically justified principles. If our farmers are to meet the challenge of feeding an ever-increasing population with a sustainable agricultural system, then they must have access to the new bio-engineered varieties. We need to think about how the WTO can help facilitate this new technology.

Developing Countries

One of the critical components to a successful new round of negotiations will be the full participation of a substantially increased number of developing countries. Open trade in agriculture relieves farmers in developing countries of the burden imposed by protectionism and export subsidies, while reducing hunger and offering reliable supplies of food at reasonable prices.

7

The Future of Agricultural Trade

In the Uruguay Round, countries recognised that the long term solution for agriculture did not lie in administered prices, trade restrictions, supply controls, and export subsidies but rather is open, nondistorted markets. It is the time to take bold steps toward bringing agricultural trade into the 21st century by accelerating agricultural trade reform.

There are four key areas for accelerating reforms: eliminating export subsidies; increasing market access though substantial tariff cuts and expansion of tariff-rate quotas; cutting further trade-distorting domestic subsidies; and ensuring technical standards are based on sound science.

The world's farmers and ranchers are facing two difficult challenges at the dawn of the 21st century. First, they are being asked to provide more products at lower cost, higher quality, greater variety, and in a safer manner than ever demanded before. Second, they are being asked to produce this abundance on a shrinking natural resources base that is often subject to government regulations. Meeting these global challenges will require unleashing the production potential of world agriculture while practising proper environmental stewardship. The ingenuity and hardwork we usually associate with farmers will be essential to meet these challenges, but they will not be sufficient unless we further reform agricultural trade to create an environment that rewards risk and investment and encourages efficiencies.

Today's Agricultural Challenges

Farmers are responsible for feeding a rapidly growing world population. And despite progress over the years, too many people still are not getting enough food. Many countries including the United States, are working vigorously to promote technological innovations to meet the need for food and fiber in the coming years. However, as important as this work is, it is only part of the solution. These technologies and the hard work of the world's farmers need a trading environment that encourages investment and efficient production, and generates economic growth to finance production and consumption needs long-term trends in agriculture pose serious challenges for all farmers. The same technological advances that increase yields may result in lower prices. Increasing social concerns about effect of agricultural production on the environment and living conditions result in new restrictions on farm activities. As urban dwellers and industry stake competing claims for land, water, and energy, many producers find their ability to farm made ever more difficult.

Two approaches to organising the agricultural economy present a stark contrast in dealing with these challenges. One model, popular in Europe and Asia, is to retain an inward-looking agricultural system focused on supply control and government regulation geared to keeping farm prices high and, since guaranteed high prices are a drain on the treasury, to controlling production. Under this approach, bureaucrats try to assess the optimal level of national production—not so little that imports are needed and not so much that excess production; must be bought at high prices and; then dumped on world markets. This 'command-and-control' structure stifles farmer efficiency and ingenuity and distorts world markets, especially as subsidised surpluses are regularly exported; and it does not address the challenge to farmers to produce food for the next century. It also ignores the interest of domestic consumers (who have to pay high internal prices) and producers in other countries (who have to compete with subsidised products). Of biggest concern is that the anti-market policies of this approach hamstring the agriculture sector from pursuing the technological advances needed to meet its future challenges.

Another approach is to place agriculture on a more market-oriented basis, particularly by removing trade barriers and reducing trade-distorting policies. Greater market orientation was the principle that actions agreed to in the last set of multilateral trade negotiations. In the Uruguay Round, countries recognised that the long-term solution for agriculture did not lie in administered prices, trade restrictions, supply controls, and export subsidies but rather in open, nondistorted markets. Now is the time to take bold steps towards bringing agricultural trade into the 21st century by accelerating agricultural trade reform.

The Gains from Trade

The benefit from free and fair trading of agricultural products have immediate effects on people. Eliminating trade barriers and reducing unfair competition will help ensure that farmers have incentives to produce and consumers have access to the products they desire. Liberalising agricultural trade will contribute to better resource allocation by farmers, which has conservation benefits, rewards low-cost producers, encourages efficiencies, and removes the drag on economic growth.

Opening trading opportunities also increases the food security of food-importing countries by giving supplier countries the confidence required to put more land into production and to create marketing relationships. Trade provides consumers with year-round access to a greater variety of less expensive products, while rewarding producers who are able to find and meet specific consumer demands for high-value products. In a broader context, by allowing imports that are more efficiently produced elsewhere, trade encourages specialisation in efficient agricultural and nonagricultural production.

More dramatically, trade literally saves lives. Without the international flow of food products from areas with abundant production to areas where food is scarce, many people in the world would be eating less or not at all. Trade has dynamic effects, as well, that push long-term productivity growth. For example, access to customers in overseas markets creates an incentive for technological innovation, resulting in exciting developments in improved seed varieties and production techniques. International markets also expand market outlets, raising prices and giving producers increased confidence to produce more than required merely for national needs, allowing productive farmers to not only feed their neighbours but literally feed the world.

Equally important, trade in agricultural products is becoming increasingly critical in farm and ranch incomes. Increased productivity and often times flat domestic demand increases the importance of reliable international markets. Foreign markets are not just a dumping ground for surplus products; overseas consumers value choice and quality, particularly when producers in their own country cannot meet their demands or when they are charged inflated prices. Consequently foreign and value-added agricultural producers, raising farm-gate prices and helping support the range of agriculture-related industries.

Political reality also encourages a focus on international markets: policies based on high government guaranteed prices are ultimately politically untenable because they are hugely expensive, unresponsive to the needs of customers and producers, incentives to environmental and agronomic realities, and a shameful waste of economic assets. Rather than farming government programmes, our producers are looking for customers around the world.

While agricultural trade benefits consumers and producers alike, it is an area in which progressive reform is ardently opposed by entrenched domestic interests. Producers in some countries, cosseted by high guaranteed prices and protective tariffs, oppose any move toward greater market orientation. Intervention in the agricultural economy—measured by the Organisation for Economic Cooperation and Development by summing price supports, direct payments, and other support as a per cent of total agricultural production—has actually increased in some countries from the levels at the beginning of the Uruguay Round. In the last set of multilateral trade negotiations, countries began the process of dismantling protection and delinking farm support from production decisions. Consequently, reforms have been undertaken by some countries.

The WTO Opportunity

The major objective in the upcoming farm talks is to accelerate the reform process initiated in the Uruguay Round. That means further substantial negotiations on tariffs, subsidies, and other trade-distorting measures so that the level and other trade-distorting measures so that the level and direction of trade are determined by market forces, not government intervention. Four key areas are outlined below:

(i) ***Export Competition:*** Export subsidies are the most distorting trade tool because the level and direction of trade is directly determined by government subsidies. Today, the European Union (EU) is the only substantial export subsidiser—nearly all other countries agreed not to use, or have only limited recourse to use, export subsidies in the last round of negotiations. EU farmers, responding to domestic prices frequently twice the world price, produce more products that can be consumed in Europe, but at such high prices that they can be sold abroad only with generous subsidies. These subsidies push other competitive suppliers out of the market (which is expensive and unfair) and discourage production in countries that have a comparative advantage in agricultural production (which is wasteful and is threatening both to the environment and to future farm production needs).

In the Uruguay Round negotiations, countries acknowledged the corrosive nature of subsidies and agreed to cap and reduce their use. The upcoming negotiations should eliminate them to ensure that countries do not resort to other policy tools that allow government spending to determine winners in the marketplace. Specifically, WTO members should look closely at curbing distorting state trading agricultural export monopolies that can disguise subsidies and exert distorting market power, along with other policies used to dispose of surplus commodities on a nonmarket basis.

(ii) ***Market Access:*** Measures applied at the border to stop trade currently are the principal barrier to a freer and more open trading environment for agriculture. Market access barriers deny efficient producers the chance to compete in other markets and limit the variety and quality of products available to consumers. Opening markets and maximising trade opportunities are fundamental principles of WTO, and we still have a long way to go in agriculture to open markets to competition.

The Uruguay Round Agreement set agricultural trade on a more predictable basis by requiring that all nontariff measures, such as quotas and import bans, be converted to simple tariffs. While this was a necessary first step to removing trade barriers, many of the tariffs are still prohibitively high. For example, while the average tariff assessed by the United States on agricultural products is less than 5 per cent (and nearly zero for industrial products), the average agriculture tariff-rate quota (TRQ). Where only specific quantities of imports receive low duties. Many other commodities also; are subject to high tariffs.

As we start the next century, higher tariffs should not stop the flow of imported agricultural products. Where TRQs remain as a transitional step before we achieve more open trade, we expect more specific disciplines on the way in which they are administered. Similarly, we need to take a hard look at agricultural state trading monopoly. Importers; use of these state traders may have been justifiable when more restrictions allowed on farm trade, but in the tariff-only regime it is hard to see why a government needs to insert itself between an exports and an end-user.

(iii) ***Domestic Subsidies:*** Domestic subsidy programmes are often the root cause of other-distorting policies. Subsidy policies that increase domestic prices above world price levels can be maintained only if price-competitive imports are restricted. Additionally, over production generated by high domestic prices can be sold on world markets only with export subsidies that bring the price down to the world price. While reining in distortive domestic subsidy programmes has value in its own right for rationalising agricultural production, the WTO negotiations will focus on their trade-distorting elements.

In the Uruguay Round negotiations, countries, agreed to distinguish trade-distorting subsidies (generally those linked to the production of a specific crop or related to price supports) from non-trade distorting subsidies (such as research and development, training and environmental production). The trade-distorting subsidies were capped, and the process of reducing allowable levels of subsidies began. This distinction is a good one: the nasty sort of subsidy that distorts markets and straitjackets producers should be cut, while programmes that will increase a country's ability to produce agricultural products in the next century without distorting production incentives should not be reduced.

(iv) ***Standards:*** As WTO members make progress on cutting tariffs and subsidies, the temptation increase to disguise trade barriers as health and safety measures or other innocuous-sounding 'technical standards'. Moreover, when regulations purportedly designed to protect health are instead vehicles for domestic protectionism, the credibility of the entire safety apparatus of a country is put up for questioning. When good science is replaced by politics, the basis for sound health policy is undermined. Therefore, increasing government accountability by putting the emphasis on sound science for health standards should discipline disguised barriers to trade and strengthen health policy.

In the Uruguay Round, countries agreed to a set of sound principles: each has the right to maintain health and safety measures, but these must be based on sound science, backed by scientific evidence and an assessment of the risk, and be no more trade-restrictive than required to meet health goals. In practice, countries have found that these principles work well—bogus measures adopted without scientific basis have been successfully challenged to the WTO without sacrificing health concerns. Creating a supportive environment for the propagation of yield-enhancing biotech products also is critical for meeting the needs of the coming century.

Agriculture is Different

Agriculture occupies a special place in the national economies of most countries around the world. Farmers are responsible for feeding and clothing people. Farming also holds a powerful claim on our national cultures that calls for the preservation of rural lifestyles and values. Farm production is subject to the cruel vagaries of weather and the relentless decline in prices and increases in costs. Some people point to these factors as justifying a different treatment for agriculture in the international economy, including justifying trade-distorting agricultural policies. This is wrong-headed; societies can support farms and preserve rural communities in ways that foster choice, protect natural resources, and expand trade.

Farm production in the next century cannot afford to be trapped in a static system in which prices are determined by government mandate, production decisions are controlled by central planners, and farmers are forced to produce only for local consumers. This myopic system cannot be sustained in any important agriculture producing society. Moreover, this type of system will not meet the needs of the coming century, when we will face unprecedented consumer demand and natural resource constraints.

Instead, I look forward to dynamic world of agricultural trade in which producers, exporters, and retailers apply the creativity of the human mind the natural bounty of the earth. In this 'new' world, we will produce a greater amount and variety of food than ever before, feed the coming billions, sustain our environment, and unlock economic resources otherwise stifled by moribund protectionism, ultimately raising living standards around the world.

8

The Uruguay Round Agreement on Agriculture

The Uruguay Round Agreement on Agriculture (URAA) calls for the initiation of negotiations for continuing the process of agricultural trade reform in 1999. Article 20 of the agreement states that member countries of the World Trade Organisation (WTO) recognise that the long-term objective of substantial progressive reductions in trade distorting support and protection of agriculture resulting in fundamental reforms is an ongoing process.

The Uruguay Round Agreement on Agriculture, which entered into force in 1995 along with other Uruguay Round accords, including the agreement to establish the World Trade Organisation, was an important step toward applying multilateral rules and disciplines to global agricultural trade. Most assessments of the agreement hail it as a historic shift in the way agriculture establishes new multilateral trade agreements. The agreement establishes new multilateral rules governing market access, export subsidies, and domestic support for agriculture. In terms of future trade liberalisation, its most important provisions may be those requiring the elimination of quantitative trade restrictions and their conversion to bound tariffs. These bound tariffs, even if some of them are extremely high, can provide a starting point for future negotiations of tariff reductions.

Market Access

The agreement requires all WTO members to convert nontariff trade barriers to tariffs and to reduce them by a simple average of 36 per cent over six years (with a minimum tariff reduction per tariff line of 15 per cent). The agreement prohibits the introduction of new nontariff barriers to trade. Where nontariff barriers restrict imports, the agreement requires that importing countries offer minimum access of usually 3 per cent of consumption rising to 5 per cent over the six-year implementation period for the agreement.

Most assessments of the agreement conclude that it provides little in the way of expanded access for agricultural products. Its importance lies in extending the principle (already applied to trade in industrial products) of protection by bound tariffs to agricultural trade and establishing at least a base for further tariff reductions in future negotiations.

Export Subsidies

The agreement requires that export subsidies be reduced by 21 per cent in terms of quantities and by 36 per cent in terms of budgetary outlays by the end of the six-year implementation period. WTO members may continue to use their existing export subsidies within the limits established, but may not introduce any new export subsidies.

Domestic Support

The agreement also includes rules and commitments for domestic support. Domestic subsidies are to be cut by 20 per cent from average levels of support aggregated across all commodities for the base period 1986-88. Support reduction commitments are also to be made over the six-year implementation period on the basis of this aggregate measure of support (AMS).

Trade policy experts contend that the rules established for domestic support policies are more important than the reduction commitments required. The agreement defines which domestic policies are permitted ('green box' policies), such as income support provided to farmers independently of participation of production-limiting programmes, advisory services, or domestic food assistance. Policies that are not eligible for the green box and automatically prohibited ('amber box' policies).

Sanitary and Phytosanitary Measures

An agreement on the Application on Sanitary and Phytosanitary (SPS) Measures reaffirms the right of WTO members to adopt and enforce measures that they deem appropriate to protect human, animal, or plant life or health as long as such measures are not applied in an 'arbitrary and unjustified' manner. The agreement states that such measures may not be used as disguised barriers to trade. SPS measures may be based on international standards where they exist. WTO members could impose higher standards than those derived from these sources if based on scientific justification and risk assessment. All WTO members agree to recognise the equivalence of different standards that result in a comparable level of SPS protection. Dispute settlement panels should seek advice from relevant international organisation when scientific or technical matters are at issue.

The SPS Agreement, though binding on WTO members, is stated in broad language. Specific will come from interpretation of the agreement and adjudication of Sanitary and Phytosanitary issues in WTO dispute settlement.

Dispute Settlement

New and strengthened dispute settlement procedures agreed to as part of the Uruguay Round also apply to disputes that may arise under either the Agreement on Agriculture or the SPS Agreement. An important change in WTO dispute settlement procedures is the elimination of a member's right to veto a dispute panel's decision and effectively block implementation of the panel's recommendations for resolving the dispute. Potentially this strengthens the ability of the WTO to enforce panel judgements. The right of WTO members to negotiate compensation rather than change its challenged policies remains in place, however.

9

The Uruguay Round and Agricultural Reforms

The Uruguay Round of Multilateral Trade Negotiations (completed in 1994) continued the process of reducing trade barriers achieved in seven previous rounds of negotiations. Among the Uruguay Round's most significant accomplishments were the adoption of new rules governing agricultural trade policy, the establishments of disciplines on the use of Sanitary and Phytosanitary (SPS) measures, and agreement on a new process for settling trade disputes. The Uruguay Round also created the World Trade Organisation (WTO) to replace the General Agreement on Tariffs and Trade (GATT) as an institutional framework for overseeing trade negotiations and adjudicating trade disputes. Agricultural trade concerns that have come to the fore since the Uruguay Round, including the use of genetically engineered products in agricultural trade, state trading, and a large number of potential new members, illustrate the wide range of issues any new round may face.

During the past years since initial implementation of the Uruguay Round agreements, the record with respect to agriculture is mixed. The Uruguay Round's overall impact on agricultural trade can be considered positive in moving toward several key goals, including reducing agricultural export subsidies, establishing new rules for agricultural import policy, and agreeing on disciplines for Sanitary and Phytosanitary trade measures. The Uruguay Round Agreement on Agriculture (URAA) may also have contributed to a shift in domestic support of agriculture away from those practices with the largest potential to affect production and, therefore, to affect trade flows. However, significant reductions in most agricultural tariffs will have to await a future round of negotiations.

Tariffs, Incentives, and Subsidies

Prior to Uruguay Round, trade in many agricultural products was unaffected by the tariff cuts that were made for industrial products in previous rounds. In the Uruguay Round, participating countries agreed to convert all nontariff agricultural trade barriers to tariffs (a process called 'tariffication') and to reduce them. However, agricultural tariffs remain very high for some products in some countries, limiting the trade benefits to be derived from the new rules. To ensure that historical trade levels were maintained and to create some new trade opportunities where trade had been largely precluded by policies, countries instituted tariff-rate quotas. A tariff-rate quota applies a lower tariff to imports below a certain quantitative limit (quota) and permits a higher tariffs on imported goods after the quota has been reached.

The Agreement on Agriculture required to reduce outlays on domestic policies that provide direct economic incentives to producers to increase resource use or production. All WTO member countries are meeting their commitments to reduce these outlays, and most countries reduced this type of support by more than the required amount. However, support from those domestic policies considered to have the least effect on production, such as domestic food aid, has increased from 1986-88 levels.

In the Agreement on Agriculture, 25 countries that employed export subsidies agreed to reduce the volume and value of their subsidised exports over a specified implementation period. To date, most of these countries have met their commitments, although some have found ways to circumvent them. The European Union (EU) is by far the largest user of export subsidies, accounting for 84 per cent of subsidy outlays of the 25 countries in 1995 and 1996. Despite substantial progress in reducing export subsidies, rising world grain supplies and falling world grain prices will make it difficult for some countries to meet future commitments unless they adopt policy changes.

The Uruguay Round's SPS agreement imposed disciplines on the use of measures to protect human, animal, and plant life and health from foreign pests, diseases, and contaminants. The agreement can be credited with increasing the transparency of countries SPS regulations and providing improved means for settling SPS-related trade disputes, including some important cases involving agricultural products. The agreement has also spurred regulatory reforms in some countries. The SPS agreement and the Agreement on Technical Barriers to Trade could provide a framework for disputes over genetically modified organisms (GMOs) brought to the WTO for arbitration.

Current Issues

Changes made to the multilateral dispute resolution process in the Uruguay Round may be as important to agricultural trade as the improvement in the substantive rules governing trade in agricultural goods. Initial evidence indicates that the WTO dispute settlement system is a significant improvement over its GATT predecessor. For example, a single country can no longer block the formation of a dispute resolution panel or veto an adverse ruling by blocking the adoption of a panel report. These improvements have led to a number of important agricultural trade cases being adjudicated before the WTO. The outstanding question for the WTO is whether members whose practices have been successfully challenged under the new dispute settlement procedures will live up to their obligations.

Other agriculture-related issues, including a bid for membership by a large and diverse group of potential new WTO members, the challenge of dealing with state trading enterprises (STEs) within WTO disciplines, and issues particular to developing countries, will shape the agenda for future agricultural trade liberalisation discussions. Thirty countries are currently seeking membership in the 134-member WTO. Countries seeking WTO membership accede under conditions negotiated with WTO membership through the privileged trade status with WTO member but may incur adjustment costs in reforming their trade policies and reducing tariffs to meet WTO requirements. Current WTO members gain greater access to the markets of acceding countries.

State trading enterprises, governmental and non-governmental entities that have been granted special rights or privileges through which they can influence trade, continue to be important to the trade of agricultural commodities because many countries consider them to be an appropriate means to meet domestic agricultural policy objectives. Continuing concerns about the trade practices of state trading enterprises in some WTO member countries and the potential accession of China and other countries where STEs are prominent will keep STEs on the WTO agenda.

Developing countries received special treatment in the Uruguay Round, including less stringent disciplines in reforming their trade policies than those apply to developed countries. In the next round of multilateral agricultural trade negotiations, developing countries will continue to have their own interests in the areas of special and differential treatment, export restraints, price stability, food security, food aid, and stock policies. As developing countries identify their positions, coalitions of countries with common trade interests may emerge.

10

Export Subsidies: A Distortion to Free Trade in Agriculture

Export subsidies are generally considered one of the most distorting trade tools used by governments to interfere with commercial markets. Export subsidies allow a government to determine the level and direction of trade solely on the basis of government subsidies, lowering world prices and denying sales for other, more competitive exporters. Not only are export subsidies unfair commercial tools, but, by encouraging surplus production, they encourage adverse environmental practices, waste government budgets, and may delay restructuring and reform of domestic industries. Substantial progress toward eliminating export subsidies will be a critical element of the World Trade Organisation (WTO) negotiations.

The Situation Today

Under the Uruguay Round Agreement, countries agreed to strictly limit the use of export subsidies. First, products that had not benefitted from export subsidies in the past were banned from receiving them in the future. Second, where countries had provided export subsidies in the past, their future use was capped and gradually reduced over 6 to 10 years. (Developed countries were required to cut their spending on export subsidies by 36 per cent over six years while also reducing subsidised export quantities by at least 21 per cent on a commodity-specific basis.

Developing countries have until 2005 to cut spending by 24 per cent and subsidised quantities by 14 per cent). Third, countries agreed not to create new schemes that serve as disguised subsidies to get around the product-specific limits. Finally, countries recognised that export credit and food aid programmes were different and exempted them from the new budget and quantity limits, although there was agreement to negotiate disciplines on export credit programmes to ensure that they do not undermine WTO commitments.

Today, the European Union (EU) is the primary export subsidizer—accounting for nearly 85 per cent of the world total. Nearly all other countries agreed in the last round of negotiations not to use or to have only limit recourse to use export subsidies. EU farmers, responding to domestic prices that are often twice the world price, produce more products than can be consumed in Europe, but at such high prices that they can be sold abroad only with generous subsidies. These subsidies force other competitors out of the market and discourage production in countries with comparative advantage.

If the EU's extravagant domestic subsidies are the root cause of export subsidies, they are also putting serious pressure on the whole EU system. The need to impose budgetary discipline on EU farm programmes (annual cost, about $46 billion) is becoming increasingly evident, even in Europe, and the EU's goal of expanding its membership to new countries in putting pressure on it to bring its farm programmes into line with other countries, which will help reduce its need to rely on export subsidies in the future.

Areas for Resolution

The upcoming negotiations should continue the work begun in the Uruguay Round and eliminate existing export subsidies. There is no economic justification for their continued use. By removing subsidised exports, world prices should increase, and farmers, particularly in the EU, will not be artificially encouraged to overproduce products that they cannot grow competitively.

In addition to eliminating export subsidies, countries should examine the rules defining export subsidies to ensure that countries do not resort to other policy tools that might allow governments to distort markets. Specially, WTO members should look closely at curbing agricultural state trading export monopolies that can exert undue market power or dispose of surplus commodities on a nonmarket basis. A recent WTO victory by the United States and New Zealand over Canada's special-class system of dairy exports shows that the existing rule against circumvention are effective but must be enforced.

Export credit and food aid programmes were addressed in the Uruguay Round agreement in recognition of the fact that those tools could be disguised as subsidies. These policies may again be on the agenda when the WTO negotiations commence next time. It will be important to ensure that the world's needy continue to have access to imported products, even when financial turmoil rolls world markets and limits the ability of developing countries to meet their food and fiber needs.

Certain large exporting nations—primarily in the EU have used export taxes as a supply management tool by intervening in the market to restrict exports when domestic stocks are low. These measures can wreak havoc in international markets, exacerbating price swings and reducing the confidence of net-food-importing countries to abandon trade barriers and rely on the international market to provide food security. Similarly, some exporting countries use differential export taxes to discourage exports of basic products (such as grains or oilseeds); they force exporters to process the product domestically (into flour or oil and meal, for example) and export the value added products.

11

WTO Agricultural Negotiations—Completing the Task

The Cairns Group of 15 agricultural-exporting countries was formed in 1986 to influence agricultural negotiations within the World Trade Organisation (WTO). It was largely as a result of the group's efforts that a framework for reform in farm products trade was established in the Uruguay Round and agriculture was for the first time subject to global trade liberalising rules. The group is positioning itself to play an important role in the new round of WTO agricultural negotiations.

The *Cairns* Group, which accounts for about 20 per cent of world agricultural exports, includes both developed and developing countries across a diverse set of regions around the world. The group consists of Argentina, Australia, Brazil, Canada, Chile, Colombia, Fiji, Indonesia, Malaysia, New Zealand, Paraguay, Philippines, South Africa, Thailand, and Uruguay. By acting collectively, this desparate group has had more influence and impact on the agriculture negotiations than individual members would have had independently. Under Australian leadership, the group takes a consensual approach to decision-making.

Beyond the Uruguay Round

Members of the Cairns Group were generally pleased with

the Uruguay Round outcome, but believe much remains to be done to ensure that a genuine market-oriented approach to agricultural policies is achieved. For example, in 1997 levels of agricultural support in Organisation for Economic Cooperation and Development (OECD) countries alone were still extremely high at $280 billion. The approach taken by the group to the challenge of reducing this assistance and creating a freer agricultural marketplace has been in two parts. First, the group has worked to ensure that countries meet the commitments that were agreed to in the agricultural-related agreements during the Uruguay Round. It has done this by remaining visible and active since the end of the round.

Second, the Cairns Group has been effective in engaging other WTO member countries in early preparation for the next round of agricultural negotiations in an attempt to ensure that they start on time and are not unnecessarily protracted as they were during the Uruguay Round. The Cairns Group in April 1998 agreed on a strongly worded 'vision statement' conveying the Group's ambition and broad objectives for the 1999 agriculture negotiations and initiated a strategic approach to the preparations for the negotiations. This approach is necessarily ambitious: "The Cairns Group of Agricultural Fair Traders reaffirms its commitment to achieving a fair and market-oriented agricultural trading system as sought by the Agreement on Agriculture. To this end, the Cairns Group is united in its resolve to ensure that the next WTO agriculture negotiations achieve fundamental reform which will put trade in agricultural goods on the same basis as trade in other goods. All trade-distorting subsidies must be eliminated and market access must be substantially improved so that agricultural trade can proceed on the basis of market forces".

Objectives for Negotiations

The vision statement outlines the Cairns Group's reform goals in three key areas within the Uruguay Round framework, as follows:

- Deep cuts to all tariffs are required, as well as the removal of tariffs peaks and the redressing of tariff escalation so that market access for agricultural commodities and value-added agricultural products is on a similar footing as trade in other commercially traded products. This should include the objective of transforming market access barriers to tariffs and removal of nontariff barriers to trade. In the interim, the Cairns Group supports substantial increases in trade volumes under tariffs-rate quotas, while the administration of tariff-rate quotas must not diminish the size and value of market access opportunities, particularly in products of special interest to developing countries.

- All trade-distorting domestic supports must be eliminated or replaced with non-trade-distorting methods of assistance. Income aids or other domestic support measures should be targeted, transparent, and fully decoupled so that they do not distort production and trade.
- Export subsidies must be made illegal for agricultural products, as they are for other traded goods, and clear rules must be established to prevent circumvention of export subsidy commitments. In this regard, it is worth nothing that only 25 of the 134 current WTO members are entitled to use export subsidies, and most of these are developed countries (with more than 80 per cent of export subsidies accounted for by the European Union). Also, agricultural export credits must be brought under effective international discipline with a view to ending government subsidisation of such credits.

Special Needs of Developing Countries

The vision statement also reaffirms the group's support for the principle of special and differential treatment for developing countries, including least-developed countries and small states, remaining an integral part of the next WTO agriculture negotiations. The Cairns Group ministers agreed that the framework for liberalisation must continue to support the economic development needs, including technical assistance requirements, of these WTO members. As has been stated by the Cairns Group, Major challenges facing many developing countries are the persistence of rural poverty and the linkages between such poverty and serious environmental problems. Consequently, more sustainable agricultural development remains a central policy issue in many developing countries. An improved international trading environment that is more conductive to supporting agricultural development is needed as an essential ingredient in addressing these problems.

Adherence to these principles will not only improve the trading environment for agricultural exporting nations, but will also have important implications for global food security. Food security will be enhanced through more diversified and reliable sources of supply, as more farmers, including poorer farmers in developing countries, are able to respond to market forces and new income-generating opportunities, without the burden of competition from heavily subsidised products. To provide further assurance to net-food-importing countries, export restrictions must not be allowed to disrupt the supply of food to world markets.

Reductions in assistance to the agricultural sector may also have positive implications for the environment. In many cases, agricultural subsidies and access restrictions have stimulated farm practices that are harmful to the environment. Reform of these policies can contribute to the development of environmentally sustainable agriculture.

Preparations for the Next Round

Cairns Group ministers welcomed the launch by the second WTO Ministerial Conference in Geneva in May 1998 of preparations for the next round of agriculture negotiations. The WTO Ministerial Declaration that emanated from this conference binds WTO members to a preparatory process that began in September 1998 and will culminate in ministerial agreement on a decision on the scope, structure, and time-frame for the agriculture negotiation.

The Cairns Group reaffirms its commitment to achieving a fair and market-oriented agricultural trading system as sought by the Agreement on Agriculture. To this end, the Cairns Group is united in its resolve to ensure that the next WTO agriculture negotiations achieve fundamental reform that will place trade in agricultural goods on the same basis as trade in other goods.

12

Developing Countries and the WTO Agricultural Negotiations

Developing countries as a group have much to gain from continued progress toward a transparent, rule-based trading system in agriculture. The researches say the negotiations should eliminate export subsidies, impose stricter disciplines on export taxes, cut tariffs, and ensure that food aid continues to be available to poor countries in grant form and delivered so as not to displace domestic production in the countries receiving it. Badly managed food aid, or cheap food imports due to export subsidies, may just reinforce the bias of economic policies against the rural sector. With its negative impact on poor agricultural producers, "they say. International research organisations (such as IFPRI, among other institutions) may provide support to developing countries through programmes of collaborative research, technical assistance and capacity strengthening.

Starting with the first found of trade negotiations under the General Agreement on Tariffs and Trade (GATT) after World War II, there has been a relatively steady trend of increasing multilateral trade liberalisation. The successive rounds of negotiations recognised the greater needs of developing countries, especially since the Tokyo Round. Yet the participation of developing countries was limited. Since many developing countries were not members of GATT, the major forum for airing their views was provided by the United Nations Conference on Trade and Development. The views of developing countries had some impact on the Lome agreements and on aid flows, but had limited influence on negotiations concerning trading rules, which were discussed within the framework of the GATT, where OECD (Organisation for Economic Cooperation and Development) countries set the agenda.

In the Uruguay Round, which began in 1986 and concluded in 1993, developing countries played a larger role in the negotiations compared to previous rounds. In particular, agricultural net exporters organised the Cairns Group (which in addition to Australia, New Zealand, and Canada, included several large developing countries such as Argentina, Brazil, Indonesia, and the Philippines) to pursue their interests. Furthermore, during and after the conclusion of the Uruguay Round, the formal accession of developing countries to the GATT and now the World Trade Organisation (WTO) has continued apace. Of the 134 members of the WTO in February 1999, some 70 per cent were developing countries. The United Nations classified 48 countries as least-developed (LLDCs): Within that group, 29 are members of the WTO, six are in the process of accession, and three are observers. Also, 18 countries have been identified as net-food-importing developing countries (NFIDCs).

Some Definitions

The LLDCs are identified by the United Nations General Assembly based on several criteria—income per capita, augmented physical quality of life index, and an index of economic diversification. As a group, they have a population of about 590 million people, with an income per capita about 4 per cent that of the world average (1996). Agricultural production per capita in LLDCs has been declining since the 1970s although the same indicator for all developing countries (mainly under the influence of China) has gone up by nearly 40 per cent in the same period. LLDCs represent a small fraction of world trade (less than 1 per cent for total and about 2 per cent for agricultural trade). They had a positive, although declining net agricultural trade balance until the mid 1980s, when it turned negative. Almost 20 per cent of their total imports are food items.

The 18 net-food-importing developing have been selected through a process within the WTO. They have a population of some 380 million people and an income per capita nearly five times that of the LLDC average, but still much lower than the world average. NFIDCs are a diverse group: four are upper-middle income countries; eight are lower-middle income; and six are lower income. Four of them had net food exports on average during 1995-97, but because they imported cereals they are included in the group. NFIDCs' per capita food production as share of both world and developing country averages has risen, although from very low levels.

Although the categories of 'developed' and 'developing' countries have important legal consequences under WTO rules, there are no formal definitions of either category. The process works through self-identification and negotiation with other member countries of the WTO.

Completing the Unfinished Agenda

In general, developing countries operate under what has been called 'special and differential treatment'. They face lower disciplines and enjoy longer time frames for implementing reforms. In the case of LLDCs, they are totally exempted from WTO commitments, and it has been agreed that developing and least-developed countries should receive special consideration for market access and technical and financial support. Also, during the Uruguay Round, concerns that liberalisation of agricultural policies and trade could adversely affect the food imports of LLDCs and NFIDCs led participants to include several measures dealing with food security issues in the 'green box' of permitted domestic support—for instance, the formation of public stockholding and the provision of foodstuffs at subsidized prices. There was a ministerial decision in Marrakesh in April 1994 to deal with possible negative effects of agricultural trade reforms on the food security of LLDCs and NFIDCs. The decision was reemphasised at the 1996 ministerial meeting of the WTO in Singapore.

Export and Domestic Subsidies: While many developing countries have significantly reduced distorting domestic agricultural policies, the possible benefits that these countries and the world can enjoy are thwarted by the subsidies of developed countries. The Uruguay Round was a first step in imposing discipline on the unfair competition arising from subsidized agricultural exports, which hurts poor agricultural producers in developing countries irrespective of their net agricultural trade position. In the next negotiations, the first step should be completed with the elimination of export subsidies. Net-food-importing developing countries should also be interested in stricter disciplines on export taxes and controls that exacerbate price fluctuations in world markets.

Under the Uruguay Round Agreement, there is still a lot of scope for the developed countries to use domestic subsidies, in addition to the use of export subsidies; to help their farmers. The developing countries should seek further disciplines in this regard, including, among other things, the elimination of exemptions under the 'blue box' (which allows farmers to receive some forms of direct payments that are considered to be trade distorting). Least-developed and developing countries, however, will still be allowed 'special and differential treatment' on these issues.

Market Access: If the developing countries are to succeed in diversifying their agricultural sectors, they need expanded access to markets in developed countries.

This includes increasing the volume of imports allowed under the current regime of tariff-rate quotas (TRQs, which replaced the previous system of rigid quotas with a combination of a quantitative quota and a high tariff for the eventual out-of-quota imports); making the administration of the TRQs more transparent and equitable; seeking further reductions in tariffs, particularly those still high in some key products; and completing the process of tariffication in the cases where exemptions were granted. Also, eliminating, or at least reducing, tariff escalation in nonagricultural products is important for developing countries: this practice undermines the possibilities of expanding production and exports of processed goods that use agricultural inputs, exploiting 'forward linkages' in the value-added chain.

What the Most Vulnerable Need

The special situation and concerns of least-developed countries and net-food-importing countries were recognised in a ministerial decision agreed upon at the completion of the Uruguay Round in 1993. These concerns include the preservation of adequate levels of food aid, the provision of technical assistance and financial support to develop the agricultural sector in those countries, and the continuation and expansion of financial facilities to help with structural adjustment and short-term difficulties in financing food imports. It is important to make food aid available in grant form, to target it to poor countries and social groups, and to deliver it in ways that do not displace domestic production in the countries receiving it. Badly managed food aid, or cheap food imports due to exports subsidies, may just reinforce the bias of economic policies against the rural sector, with its negative impact on poor agricultural producers.

Volatility in agricultural prices must be monitored carefully. While expansion of world agricultural trade should limit overall fluctuations by spreading supply and demand shocks over larger areas, the decline in world public stocks as a percentage of consumption works in the opposite direction. Improving early warning of potential food shortages, lowering costs for food transportation and storage, and providing better targeted food aid programmes and financial facilities for emergencies are also issues that need to be addressed by countries participating in the coming round of negotiations.

The impact of changes in trade and agricultural policy on poorer consumers and producers in developing countries is a matter of debate. Some have argued that trade liberalisation may hurt both groups. Others have answered that greater productivity and growth coming from better trade and sectoral policies should help generate employment and income, given a setting of adequate overall economic policies and properly functioning markets and social institutions.

Small producers will also be helped by the disciplines that the URAA is bringing to subsidised and dumped exports, while it allows the implementation of a variety of programmes aimed at poor producers or consumers, including stocks for food security purposes and domestic food aid for populations in need. The issue here is the adequate design and funding of domestic policies to achieve the intended objectives of agricultural growth and poverty alleviation, which most certainly will not be helped by trade-distorting interventions either in developed or developing countries.

In general, low-income developing countries and LLDCs should emphasize to the international community the importance of creating and expanding a supportive international trade and financial environment and of implementing an integrated framework for economic and social development, with agricultural and trade policies being an integral part of the strategy. Appropriate measures would include—in addition to the agricultural trade issues suggested here—the continuation and enhancement of the reduction of the external debt of Heavily Indebted Poor Countries (the HIPS initiative) and the further liberalisation of trade in textiles.

But improved international conditions should go hand-in-hand with a better domestic framework in developing and least-developed countries, including stable macroeconomic policies, open and effective markets, good governance, the rule of law, a vibrant civil society, and programmes and investments that expand opportunities for all, with special consideration for poor and disadvantaged groups.

Bringing Developing Countries into the Process

Developing countries, as small players in the global arena, should be interested and active participants in the design and implementation of international rules that limit the ability of larger countries to resort to unilateral action. Also, domestic legal and institutional frameworks in developing countries may be strengthened by the implementation of internationally negotiated rules that limit the scope for rent seeking and arbitrary projectionist measures. The developing countries as a group have much to gain from continued progress toward a transparent, rule-based, trading system in agriculture.

What are the requirements and skills for the developing countries to become effective members in the next WTO round? Any negotiation requires careful consideration of the legal, economic, and political dimensions that define the substance and possible evolution of the negotiations, as well as the diplomatic and negotiating techniques that may help in the attainment of the expected outcomes. Questions that need to be addressed include:

- What are the economic and social consequences of different WTO scenarios (quantitative estimation of impacts)? Knowing the impacts of alternative scenarios is crucial if developing countries are to represent their interests in the negotiation process;
- What are the legal issues being discussed (definition of obligations, exemptions, time frame, and so on)? Detailed knowledge of international trade law is crucial if developing countries are not to be 'shortchanged'. The devil is in the details;
- Looking at the political process, who are the main actors and their interests and what type of alliances may drive the negotiations? Negotiators must understand the political economy of their own country and of other countries in the WTO if they are to negotiate effectively;
- With these elements, an adequate diplomatic and negotiating strategy must be defined and implemented.

Developing countries that have carefully considered all four components will be better prepared to participate effectively in the coming negotiations. Of course, limited financial and human resources act as an important constraint. However, developing countries may overcome some of the problems through collective action, for instance considering the creation of alliances with respect to their main export and import commodities and the markets they approach for their exports. An example is the Cairns Group. This approach could reduce the fixed costs of negotiations. Spreading them over groups of countries, allow a better use of scarce technical expertise, and improve the bargaining position of developing countries. It could also be in the interest of the OECD countries to deal with negotiating blocs, which represent a smaller number of negotiating positions, rather than with numerous separate countries. The negotiations would be much more efficient and balanced.

13

Population Growth and Cropland

Since mid-century, global population has grown much faster than the cropland area. The trend is likely to continue in the next century, dropping cropland per person to historically low levels. The ever smaller per capita cropland base will make food self-sufficiency impossible for many countries, and will test the capacity of international markets to meet a growing demand for imported food.

For millennia, farmers satisfied rising food demand by bringing new land under the plow. But by mid-century cropland expansion could no longer meet the food needs of an increasingly populous and prosperous world. The 10,000 year era of steady expansion was over, and a new era began that stressed raising land productivity. As this high-yielding era shows signs of faltering, concern over the shrinking supply of cropland per person looms ever larger.

Since mid-century, grain area—which serves as a proxy for cropland in general—has increased by some 19 per cent, but global population has grown 132 per cent, seven times faster. Largely, as a result, grain area per person has fallen by half since 1950, from 0.24 to 0.12 hectares. Assuming that grain area remains constant, grain area per person will fall to 0.07 hectares by 2050. In crowded industrial countries such as Japan, Taiwan, and South Korea, grain area per capita today is smaller than the area of a tennis court.

As grain area per person falls, more and more nations risk losing the capacity to feed themselves. Having already seen per capita grain area shrink by 40-50 per cent between 1960 and 1998, Pakistan, Nigeria, Ethiopia, and Iran can expect a further 60-70 per cent loss by 2050—a conservative projection that assumes no further losses of agricultural land. The result will be four countries with a combined population of more than 1 billion whose grain area per person will be only 300-600 square metres, less than a quarter of the area in 1950.

The historical record suggests that such a small area per person will send a substantial share of a country's people to world markets from their food. Consider the experience of six countries in East Asia whose per capita grain area currently ranges from 200 to 600 square metres per person. Sri Lanka relies on imports for more than a third of its grain, while Japan, Thiwan, South Korea, and Malaysia buy more than 70 per cent of their grain from abroad. North Korea is the only one of the six that does not import heavily (it gets less than 20 per cent of its grain requirements from abroad), but its population is poorly fed—indeed, on the verge of starvation.

The concern is that population growth will push many nations—not just the four fastest-growing ones—below the 600-square metre-threshold in coming decades. In Asia alone, where grain area per person stands at 800 square metres, 16 countries are poised to cross this threshold by 2050, and many of them much sooner. As this process unfolds, the number of people who will turn to foreign markets for their food will likely jump sharply. These countries will find an increasingly tight international grain market, with nations from the Middle East, North Africa, and other regions already buying a third or more of their grain overseas.

In addition to per capita losses, population growth can lead to degradation of cropland, reducing its productivity or even eliminating it from production. As a country's population density increases and good farmland becomes scarce, poor farmers are forced onto ecologically vulnerable land such as hillsides and tropical forest. In the Philippines, for example, hillside agriculture accounted for only 10 per cent of all agricultural land in 1960, but 30 per cent in 1987. Because it is highly erodible, hillside land is easily damaged; worldwide, some 160 million hectares of hillside farmland—11 per cent of cropland—were characterised in 1989 as 'severely eroded'. Similarly, population pressure can force peasants to overfarm the poor soils of tropical forests. After being cleared and farmed for a new years, these soils typically require fallow periods of 20-25 years, but population pressures keep poor farmers on the same land for far longer than the soil can support, cutting fallow periods to just a few years in some areas of tropical Africa and Asia.

Finally, population pressures on a fixed base of land can result in rural landlessness. In Bangladesh, for example, landlessness among rural households rose from 35 per cent in 1960 to 53 per cent in the early 1990s. Interestingly, Bangladesh is regarded as a success in slowing population expansion, as its growth rate declined from 2.8 per cent in the late 1970s to 1.5 per cent in the early 1990s. But its success came too late to prevent the increase in rural landlessness, highlighting the need to work sooner, rather than later, for population stabilisation.

14

Development of Sericulture

In majority of the developing nations, development efforts in the last decade were put on hold. In all the developing nations, poverty is on rise, economic growth has slowed down, employment has faltered and inflation is on upward swing. A greater proportion of the population in these countries depends on agriculture sector for their livelihood. But, in agriculture sector productivity is low. This is not only because of excess pressure on land but also agriculture in these developing nations is characterised by primitive technologies, poor organisation and limited capital.

Since the urban growth is severely limited, the growing labour forces have to get their employment in the rural areas or semi-urban areas in the coming decades. So, it has become compulsory for the agriculture sector to share the increasing burden since it is the major activity for the majority of the labour force.

It is obvious that in India larger than the necessary number of workers needed in agriculture are working on limited resources. As a result, agriculture sector has become an unprofitable activity with low levels of productivity. Moreover, the traditional crops have failed to absorb the growing labour force and to raise the incomes of the farmers above the subsistence level.

Since agriculture has been considered as the backbone of Indian economy, Indian agriculture can be broadly classified under two categories—*(i)* rainfed or dryland farming and *(ii)* irrigated farming. Rainfed agriculture is primarily rain dependent. Rainfed agriculture in India supports 40 per cent of the total cultivated area. As irrigation facilities are inadequate, agriculture is still a gamble in the hands of monsoons.

For most of the irrigation projects, rainfall is the only source. Due to erratic nature of rainfall, most of the dams, tanks and other water reservoirs remain dry during summer season. These rainfed areas are frequently affected by periodic droughts, soil erosion, crop fluctuations and other related problems. To overcome these problems, the Government of India has implemented such projects which are helpful for eradication of poverty and unemployment and upliftment of the weaker sections.

In this context suitable strategies are needed to overcome the above mentioned problems. The discovery of productive employment opportunities in the integrated rural development assumes vital importance in the economic development of India. So, it is natural to start with agriculture as the biggest of India's industries. The most important method of securing an increase in agriculture output is by inducing the cultivators to adopt better agricultural practices.

In fact, Indian agriculture now is no longer confined to the cultivation of traditional crops. The farmers are encouraged to take up agriculture practices which are integrated with live-stock culture, animal husbandry, dairying, fisheries, poultry, horticulture and sericulture to generate more income for each household.

In spite of the limitations in agriculture, it can be said without any doubt that Indian agriculture is on the threshold of entering into a stage of development characterised by a shift from static technology to a modern technology, in which capital requirement and purchased inputs occupy a larger share. But, much of the success of new programmes will depend upon the ability of the workers who act as growth promoters.

It is in this context, sericulture with its vast potential for employment generation in rural areas plays a vital role in alleviating rural poverty. However, this is another crop enterprise which is identified as one of the most appropriate labour intensive cottage industries. This activity combines both agriculture and industry. It provides gainful employment not only at the stage of raising of mulberry plants but also at the stage of rearing of silk worms using output of the farmers as an input of the latter. Sericulture, for example, played a very important role in transforming the traditional bound Japanese agriculture into a modernised agriculture by intensive use of land, labour and capital.

Now, in India sericulture has become the most promising rural activity due to certain specific reasons like minimum gestation period, less investment, maximum employment potential and quick turnover of the investment. Sericulture generates direct and indirect employment in various ways. First, mulberry cultivation creates employment on the farm and secondly cocoon production which uses mulberry leaves as an input creates large-scale employment for the family labour of the mulberry growers, if that operation is also undertaken by the same household to reduce their underemployment in agriculture. Further, the reeling activity is also mainly undertaken in rural areas or semi-urban areas and the employment generated there would help to reduce the rural unemployment in a significant way. In short, sericulture as a whole, by its very nature of activities creates large scale employment and income generation opportunities in the rural and nearby semi-urban areas accelerating the economic growth of these areas.

Details of Sericulture Development in Kurnool District of A.P.

Sericulture is better suited for drought prone areas. Kurnool district is one among the frequently drought affected district of

Rayalaseema and suitably sericulture finds its place. Sericulture was first introduced in the district during 1975-76 in Bapananthapuram village of Atmakur Mandal. The area under mulberry was gradually increased over the years to 10,000 acres covering almost in all mandals in the district upto 1990 and the area stood at all time high in 1990. But in the subsequent years the net area got reduced because of large scale uprooting by existing farmers due to losses suffered by them an account of steep fall in cocoon price and outbreak of deadly chronic disease in 1991/92 scanty erratic rains and continuous dry spell also major factors for uprooting. However due to its lucrative income the area under mulberry is developed. Now the district is self sufficient and even supplying seed cocoon to neighbouring districts. As far non-farm sector in sericulture in the district one 6 basin multi-end silk reeling unit. One 6 basin silk reeling unit and 40 country charkas and a complex of 100 Twin Charkas are established in private sector. As many as 300 silk looms are functioning in Adoni area.

Item	*1994-95*	*1995-96*	*1996 97*	*1997-98*	*1998-99*	*1999-2000*	*2000 to 2001 as on 1/2001*
Area under mulberry cultivation acres	4930	5273	5141	4232	5115	4195	3952
Cocoon production (in tonnes)	882	895	967	924	107	7.66	6.15
Qty. of raw silk Produced both in Pvt. and Govt. sectors (in tons)	2.23	2.2	3.8	6.0	3.3	3..3	4.3
	2450	2649	2774	2386	2558	2131	1935

Infrastructure Facilities Available in the District

Govt. Sector

1.	Tech. Service Centres (Extension)	:	7 Nos. (Atmakur, Pamulpadu, M. Lingapuram, Nandyal, Nandikotkur, Adoni and Pathikonda
2.	Tech. Service Center (Non-farm)	:	1 No. (Atmakur)
3.	Govt. Silk Reeling Unit	:	1 No. (Kurnool)
4.	Silk Worm Egg Production Centres	:	2 Nos. (Atmakur, Nandyal)
5.	Govt. Seed Farms	:	5 Nos. (Peapully, Kalichetla, Venkatapuram, Gajulapalli and Thangadancha)
6.	Seed Areas	:	2 Nos. (Adoni, Peapully)
7.	Govt. Seed Cocoon Market	:	1 No. (Adoni)
8.	Govt. CB Cocoon Market	:	1 No. (Atmakur)

Private Sector

1.	Pvt. Charkas	:	4 Nos. Nandikotkur, Atmakur
2.	Silk Twisting Units	:	4 Nos. Yemmiganur, Kodumur Nandikotkur and Nandyal
3.	Silk Power Loom Units	:	1 No. Yemmiganur
4.	Silk Looms	:	3118 Nos. Kodumur, Yemmiganur, Adoni, Pathikonda, Koilakuntla, Nandavaram
5.	Silk Weavers Co-op Society	:	1 No. Gudikal (with 40 looms)

Details of Loans and Subsidies (Credit Flow)

Sl. No.	*Item*	*1996-97*		*1997-98*		*1998-99*		*1999-2000*	
1.	Loan	23.7	17.80	2.61	–	0.69	–	–	–
2.	Subsidy	8.78	7.13	5.12	–	0.46	–	–	–
3.	Margin money	–	1.78	–	–	–	–	–	
	Total	**32.50**	**26.7**	**7.73**	–	**1.15**	–	–	–

Achievements under VIII Plan

Provided 100 House-cum-work-sheds for Charka silk reeling to the rural poor people.

Proposals under IX Plan

(a) Providing rearing sheds on 50 per cent subsidy to Seed Farms by CSB

(b) Providing Drip irrigation to Mulberry gardens of sericulturists

(c) Establishment of Multiend silk reeling machines.

Women Development Programme

Sl. No.	*Year*	*Programme*	*Physical*	*Financial*
1	2	3	4	5
1.	1995-96	1. Women Farmers meet	350	
		2. Women Groups	02	
		3. Thrift-cum-Credit Group	02	
2.	1996-97	1. Study Tours	125	0.4375
		2. Try in Mulberry Cultivation's and SW Rearing	25	0.1125
		3. Women groups	02	0.05

(Contd...)

1	2	3	4	5
3.	1997-98	1. Try to Women Sericulturists in New Technologies	75 –	0.225 –
		2. Women Groups	01	0.25
4.	1998-99	1. Trg. to Women Sericulturists in New Techniques	30 –	0.30 –
		2. Women Groups	01	0.25
5.	1999-2000	Nil	–	–
6.	2000-2001	Nil	–	–

Trends in Employment under Sericulture

Year	*No. of persons engaged in sericulture*
1995-96	19076
1996-97	20564
1997-98	16928
1998-99	20460

Cocoons Markets in the District

1. Atmakur : CB Cocoon Market
2. Kurnool : Notified Cocoon Market
3. Adoni : Seed Cocoon Market

Transactions made in Govt. Cocoon Markets

Year	*Qty. of Cocoons sold*	*Market fee collected*	*Total value realised*
1995-96	5429	11904	566744
1996-97	6973	17518	822714
1997-98	11748	25892	1294000
1998-99	4458	8276	489000
1999-2000	137390	28999	1449886
2000-2001	1034	20463	1271947

15

Controlling the Global Tobacco Epidemic Towards a Transnational Response

Recent trends in the globalisation of the tobacco industry are reflected in the shifting of the burden of tobacco-related disease and deaths towards developing countries. Tobacco companies have proved sufficiently powerful to thwart comprehensive control programmes in all but a handful of countries. What new strategies are needed to control the epidemic in developing regions?

One billion people smoke worldwide and around 3.5 million die from tobacco-related illness annually. By 2030, this figure will rise to ten million, with 70 per cent of deaths in lower and middle income countries (LMICs). Four companies now control 75 per cent of global cigarette sales, as sophisticated strategies for supply, production and sales have produced increasingly popular global brands.

The onward march of Marlboro man epitomises this globalisation, exploiting the opportunities presented by trade liberalisation, regional organisations and the communications revolution. Control efforts are undermined by the industry's success in developing favourable relationships with many governments, the magnitude of their foreign direct investments and the scale of advertising, marketing and sponsorship campaigns. In addition, large-scale cigarette smuggling, which comprises one-third of total exports, depletes tax revenues and further jeopardises public health.

A unique response by the World Health Organisation (WHO) reflects the scale of the challenge. WHO is negotiating its first public health treaty: the Framework Convention on Tobacco Control. To be effective, this potentially powerful instrument must be backed up by strengthened national policies set within the context of globalisation and based on an appreciation of transnational tobacco industry strategies. In support of this process, an international team based at the London School of Hygiene and Tropical Medicine carried out pilot studies in Thailand and Zimbabwe. These aimed to initiate the development of guidelines for tobacco policy research in LMICs, where resources and expertise are frequently lacking.

The political sensitivities surrounding tobacco control reflect the complex array of powerful vested interests involved. The case studies showed that political mapping and stakeholder analysis can make a valuable contribution to understanding the opportunities and constraints for national control policies in an era of globalisation. For example, they found that the 1992 Global Agreement on Tariffs and Trade (GATT) ruling that opened Thailand's previously closed cigarette market had contradictory results:

- Thailand is a key market for tobacco companies seeking expansion in Asia.
- The US Trade Representatives secured access to the Thai market through GATT's insistence on equal treatment of domestic and foreign cigarette manufacturers, and imports escalated rapidly.
- The GATT ruling also upheld the right to protect public health, giving a major impetus to health activists pressing the Thai government for action.

- Subsequent comprehensive control legislation has stabilised smoking rates in Thailand.

Control policies of wealthier countries cannot simply be transplanted to poorer nations. Knowledge of the complex policy environments surrounding tobacco control in LMICs is limited and effective policies will require.

- Detailed analysis of the particular political and economic contexts.
- Multidisciplinary expertise from public health and social science.
- Links between researchers, policymakers and activists.
- Support for national research capacity through the development of clear guidelines for tobacco policy analysis and their application by national researchers.

Finally, the enforced opening of internal industry documents provides an important new resource. Access to the depositories in Minnesota, USA, and Guildford, UK, and via the internet offers a unique opportunity to understand the global strategies of the tobacco companies. Analysis of their contents has so far focused on the United States. There is an urgent need to extend this attention to industry activities within LMICs.

16

Land Tenure

Securing Land for the Urban Poor

Around the world, especially in Asia and Africa, towns and cities are expanding rapidly. For the poorest people, finding, affordable, safe and secure urban land for shelter has become increasingly difficult. This is because:

- overall competition for land makes it increasingly costly;
- central urban areas are being developed for commercial use;
- natural features such as mountains or swamps limit physical urban expansion; and
- meeting land management and planning standards (concerned with legality, technical and administrative accuracy) is expensive.

As a result, a large and increasing proportion of urban populations are forced to live in peripheral areas or occupy marginalised and dangerous locations. These settlements are often illegal and, providing inadequate shelter and lacking essential services, only exacerbate the problems of the poor. Higher levels of ill health, unemployment and non-sustainable land-use often result. Furthermore, residents may also be under constant threat of eviction by government, and exploitation by landowners.

Experience shows that, if residents in such areas feel secure and safe from eviction, they do over time improve their neighbourhoods. Recognition of and granting of secure forms of tenure of previously illegal settlements often provides the incentive to communities to invest their resources in upgrading their housing and wider neighbourhoods. Security of tenure also brings the improved likelyhood of basic infrastructure and other essential community services.

There is a wide range of urban land tenure systems. In many urban areas, including areas designated illegal by government, there are informal or customary tenure systems—these are often the commonest form of tenure and are expanding most rapidly.

While statutory or 'legal' forms of tenure (for example freehold or leasehold agreements) offer many advantages, such as full individual rights and security and access to formal credit systems, they can also cause the very problems they were intended to solve:

- Higher rental levels, which may displace existing renters;
- The selling out of the secure land to higher income groups;
- Encouragement of new illegal/informal settlements, as the poorest hope that they will also eventually get security of tenure;
- Encouragement of landowners and developers to hold land, without investing in its improvement or paying taxes on its increased value—which serves to attract even greater levels of investment and land price inflation.

In addition, if people's incomes remain low and the capacity of the banks or credit unions is weak, statutory forms of tenure alone may not necessarily stimulate neighbourhood improvements.

Consequently, careful analysis of existing systems of informal and customary tenure and property rights is required, before embarking on major land management and tenure reforms. These can provide both acceptable levels of security and access to credit, which in turn stimulate improvements to local neighbourhoods. Before any decisions are made, tenure policies must recognise the likely impact on tenants, the poor and other vulnerable groups, especially women.

For these reasons, it is sometimes better to increase the rights of residents (*e.g.* by protecting them from the threat of forced evictions, or by increasing their access to essential utilities or credit), rather than assuming that they need freehold or leasehold titles.

Strategies for providing shelter now recognise the diverse nature of needs, and the positive contribution which decent housing makes to social and economic development at both national and local levels. They also recognise that the most effective way of mobilising the resources required is to encourage investment in housing by individuals, communities and the private sector.

Recent experience shows that many governments are now introducing positive approaches which are market-sensitive and encourage more efficient use of available land. These include measures to encourage landowners and developers to allocate a specified proportion of units to low-income groups out of profits generated from planning permission granted by (and therefore partly created by) the government. Public-private partnerships and revisions to planning standards and administrative procedures have also demonstrated that it is possible to reduce the costs of access to land for the poor even under conditions of market-led development, thus reducing urban sprawl, the occurrence of slum settlements and levels of poverty.

17 Can Economic Growth Reduce Poverty?

New Findings on Inequality, Economic Growth and Poverty

Many people still think first of 'economic growth' in relation to poverty reduction. Indeed, their correlation is one of the most-discussed issues of combating poverty. The relationship is of great importance because if there is a clear causal dependency, reducing poverty could fundamentally be limited to measures to promote growth. However, if there was low growth or stagnation it would not be possible to reduce poverty decisively. In the opposite case, that of the phenomena having no causal relation, promising measures to reduce poverty could be taken up even without economic growth.

Hardly anyone now explicitly expresses the view that economic development trickles down automatically to the poor. Practical experience has refuted this assumption dating from the early days of development policy in the 1960s. However, a number of studies show development of growth and a decline in poverty running parallel. On the other hand, there are also examples which show that despite high economic growth, poverty is not reduced markedly. The common answer to the question this raises is thus: Yes, growth can reduce poverty, but only if additional measures oriented on the poor are taken up.

This is often termed pre-poor-growth. But what that means in detail, and whether economic growth as such plays a causal role at all, is not clarified. It is worth taking a look at the arguments on the basis of more recent empirical and theoretical knowledge.

No Direct Causality between Growth and Poverty Reduction

Among the many indicators of poverty, the income of the poor (income poverty) has the closest relationship to economic growth. An increase in gross domestic product and thus national income could, if other factors come into play be linked with an increase in the per capita income of the poor.

Such a relationship between economic growth and the income of the poor, however, cannot be described as causal, as in asserted implicitly time and again by the statement that growth is a necessary but not sufficient precondition for poverty reduction. In so far as growth and poverty reduction arise at the same time at the end of a process, they exist alongside each other. It would be almost a tautology to say that the former is the cause or part-cause of the latter. Both express the same thing, namely a change in per capita income as well, and both have similar causes. What matters is recognising what these causes are and what specific factors must come into play so that the income of the poor grows too. Growth as a 'prerequisite' or 'condition' is then no longer the focus; the priority is asking for specific policies that result in higher incomes for the poor. The detour in thinking about growth is not necessary. Since, however, it is based on similar factors, such as fiscal policy/budget structure, employment policy, combating inflation, and institutional development, economic growth can also emerge if poverty is reduced. The difference of views lies in the fact that under the heading 'poverty reduction' the aim is no longer growth, but a purposeful reduction of poverty.

Therefore, in reverse, successful combating of poverty can be seen as being the cause of growth insofar as activating the capabilities of the poor and using their productive capacity of the poor and using their productive capacity triggers economic drive.

Indirect Causality between Growth and Poverty Reduction?

So even if economic growth fundamentally has no direct causal impact on poverty, growth still can reduce it indirectly. This is the case when due to positive economic development a government has greater revenue and uses the surplus for combating poverty, for example by providing such public goods as education and health services. Also in these cases, however, growth is not a compelling precondition. Even without growth greater government revenue can be achieved for example by more efficient tax collection. And leeway for social welfare spending can be gained by redistributing the budget, such as by cutting military appropriations. Furthermore, an automatic process is not given because the government can also use surplus funds for non-social purposes.

Creation of jobs due to increased economic activity can be another indirect link between economic growth and income poverty, if such a development generates income and reduces poverty. But also in this case I see no compelling, causality because, for instance, industrial jobs are not necessarily open to the really poor. In addition, these positive impacts occur to a considerable extent only in the event of labour-intensive development. In many countries, however, economic growth is achieved by capital-intensive production.

Inequality, Growth and Income Poverty

If national incomes, grow, a naïve observer might assume that the income of the poor must also grow along with it. But that would be a statistical fallacy. Even if only the income of the rich grows, this results in macroeconomic statistics showing a higher per capita income. What the true conditions are, is shown as soon as one divides the production statistically into income groups, such as in fifths, as is usual. It then turns out that the bald figures on average per capita growth can certainly cloak a situation where the income of the richest fifth of the population is growing fast while that of the poorest fifth is stagnating. Despite growth, the gap between the two becomes even wider.

The unequal distribution of income (and of other assets such as property and access to social services), and its connection to poverty reduction and growth has recently returned to the forefront of the debate.

It is obvious that inequality and its changes have direct effects on the poverty situation. Does inequality also have an impact on poverty via its relation to growth, because growth promotes or reduces inequality? Earlier, the predominant view was that rapid growth was linked with at least a temporary increase in inequality, so that a distinct policy of growth initially disadvantaged the poor.

The current dominant view is that growth has no foreseeable effects on inequality and that inequality changes only very slowly, in reverse, however, it is assumed that greater equality is a determinant of growth. According to that view, an indirect relationship between poverty on one side and inequality as a factor dependent upon growth on the other is not given.

That leads to the conclusion that fair distribution has more weight than growth. Fair distribution, however, does not depend upon growth. An appropriate policy is possible at any time, not only after an economic situation has improved. The notion that still shimmers through the debate that "something must be earned first before it can be distributed" is wrong. It is a matter of designing policy and the entire economic process right from the start in such a way that the surplus benefits all including the poor. Important elements of such a policy are, for example, land reform and development of finance systems.

Relationship of Growth to Poverty

According to today's conventional wisdom, income poverty expresses only a part of what poverty means. Not least through the voices of the poor themselves, it has become clear that violation of human dignity and rights, a lack of participation in decisions and exclusion from society, unequal treatment of men and women, and vulnerability are also regarded as poverty. For poverty is caused to a great degree by conflicts of power and interests. Income poverty often is not even seen as the greatest problem.

What relationship do these more far reaching characteristics of poverty have to economic growth? A direct relationship of growth to socially-related aspects such as women's inheritance rights, land rights and exclusion from decisions cannot be seen. Considerable improvements in favour of the poor can be achieved here even without economic growth.

Those who see a strong and causal connection between economic growth and poverty reduction must ask themselves what the prospects are for high growth rates and thus for a decline in poverty. Coupling poverty reduction to economic growth is problematic. If only low growth rates are to be expected.

Another question is whether continuous increases in growth are at all desirable and possible in the medium to long term. In this connection, a difference should perhaps be made between developing countries and industrialised nations. But environmental compatibility and availability of resources set limits to growth for both. Some academics assume that industrialised nations have already reached an inherent limit (stagnation theory) and that the high growth rates of earlier years will not return. Moreover, they add, full employment is no longer achievable due to, among other things, an ongoing increase in productivity, and current unemployment cannot be reduced by customary means. In any case, if growth were to be taken as the major benchmark, the prospects for a radical reduction of income poverty around the world would be modest.

Summing Up

Poverty is a complex problem and reducing it depends upon many interconnected factors, that is why poverty cannot be attributed to one main cause nor its reduction based on one main strategy. Economic growth is just one strategic element among many others related to poverty reduction. An indirect causal connection between growth and poverty reduction can only be seen because governments will have a greater scope for action due to economic growth, and if they promote labour-intensive development.

Therefore growth's role in poverty reduction must be put into perspective Growth cannot be the first thing that comes to mind, nor is it is the golden path to reducing poverty. The simplistic theory of economic growth as the main condition obstructs the bigger picture; to clings to the underlying and ongoing belief in the trickle-down effect. Even if there is no growth or for inherent reasons there can be none, there are promising ways to take on the challenge of mass poverty in the developing countries. Up front, governments and bilateral and multilateral donors must have the political will to design economic, financial and social policies so that they are oriented on poverty in a coherent way—the result can also be economic growth.

18

The Dynamics of Rural Poverty in India

Poverty is homogeneous only when considered from the point of view of income or consumption: the uniformity of the poor as a category exists only on the level of the fact that they have little to consume. When considered from the point of view of production, *i.e.*, the circumstances in which the poor must operate to gain their income, the conditions of poverty are extraordinary diverse. A concrete grasp of these diverse circumstances is the first step in developing relevant instruments to address not only the problems of the poor, but also the challenge of taking advantage of the opportunities available to them.

The conventional means of measuring economic progress, such as Gross National Product per capita, tell us little about the real nature of poverty. In recent years this sort of yardstick has been supplemented by measurements of food security, income distribution, and social development (encompassing health and education). These offer the possibility of composite indices, allowing the development of more rounded characterizations and comparisons of poverty at the national level. However, these principally refer to the symptoms of poverty, not to the relational factors generating it. Poverty is not a state of being, it is the effect of dynamic processes. While it is important to know where poverty is greatest, it is critical to know why it exists. This inquiry necessarily leads away from the nature of the poor as individuals to the nature of their social and physical environment. Poverty is not only a personal phenomenon, it is a social status. As such, while its effects can be measured on the level of the individual, its causes must be sought elsewhere. From the point of view of poverty alleviation the process of becoming is just as important as the state of being.

At the heart of poverty is the inadequate access of the poor to productive resources. Low incomes tend to reflect inadequate means of production, not incompetent producers. However, poverty in India is not simply a reflection of private resources. A broad range of 'external' factors impinge on incomes, among them the following:

National Policies

One of the ironies of Indian development is that while no government wants poverty, many policies contribute to it—what is given in anti-poverty programmes is drained away by other policies. The poor do not always come out ahead in the balance—they are often net 'donors' to the rest of society. Frequent reference is made to unsustainable forms of development—to urban over-expansion, industrialisation based on subsidies, and to public sector engorgement. What is less frequently realised is that the bill for these phenomena is often presented to the rural poor. Taxation of exports to sustain sectors with little export potential of their own and subsidised food imports to supply the urban population are policies that are often paid for by the rural poor. In many areas of India, exports are agricultural goods produced by small farmers. Here export taxes contribute to rural poverty. The same is true of 'cheap' food imports which depress the prices paid to small farmers for their food crops.

Structural imbalance' is not only a recipe for increasing external indebtedness, it is also a recipe for increasing the poverty of the rural population. The political weakness of the poor in most areas is not only the basis for inadequate poverty alleviation programmes and policies—it is the basis for an actual transfer of their income to more socially influential groups. While it is often correctly asserted that the poor are the first to suffer from adjustments involving public social expenditure cuts, it is often the case that they also have the most to gain from the elimination of policy-based economic distortions that reflect social power rather than productive efficiency and potential.

Demographic Factors

Accelerated population growth is a long-term contributor to poverty. In India the incomes of the poor have declined, mortality rates are also falling, pushing the numbers up. In the meantime, land is becoming scarcer, plots more fragmented and the soil and pasture increasingly degraded. This phenomenon is not without its policy dimensions. As long as the poor remain undercapitalised, and essential determinant of household income is the amount of labour available to it household economic strategies favour large families. While population policy has a role to play, possibly more critical is a change in the economic environment. Access to capital and more secure income changes perceptions of the need for labour. In the medium-and long-term, population dynamics are driven by the underlying productive systems. As long as the production systems of the poor remain underdeveloped, population growth remains high, restricting even the future possibility of development.

Natural Resource Management and the Environment

If poverty is both cause and effect of rapid population expansion, so poverty is both cause and effect of many dimensions of degradation of the environment. Many of the rural poor, but by no means all, live in areas of extreme environmental fragility, a circumstance often prompted by high level of control by the better-off over more stable and productive resource areas. Here the poor are extraordinarily exposed to the dangers of erosion, whittling away at an already meager productive base. The threat is not entirely due to nature. Rather, poverty accelerates erosion. Without capital, the poor are frequently unable to invest in even traditional methods of soil and water conservation. And without sufficient land they are forced to shorten fallow periods, putting further strain on the resource base. As in the case of population growth, the result is strain not only on the poor, but on the entire Indian economy. Given the extremely limited economic alternatives, the solution to this problem is not to forbid the use of environmentally fragile resources to the poor, it is to change the conditions under which their use takes place. Access to conservation technology is important, but more so are security of land tenure and resources to invest.

Combating poverty means not only increasing the production of the poor, but also preserving and enhancing the long-term value of the resource they control. What this very often means, in practice is assisting the poor in reestablishing a stable relationship with fragile resource. Prevailing processes in many areas involve the gradual—and sometimes not so gradual—depletion of natural resources, to the detriment of all. Part of the answer to this is conservation. Part of the answer is also to provide viable economic alternatives to the poor, reducing their dependence on erosion-prone crop and livestock practices.

Exploitative Intermediates

The poor are not unaware of the pressure upon them, and also of means of overcoming them. Their ability to respond, however, is severely impaired by social powerlessness. The poor are surrounded by a dense network of public and private factors reducing their freedom of action, and actually draining what few resources they do have. Members of the network include traders and moneylenders capitalising upon the economic weakness of the poor, and engaging them in unequal exchanges. They also include public agencies either indifferent to the requirements of the socially uninfluential, or actively engaged in extracting 'surplus' for use by other groups. Not to be excluded from this are organisations which are ostensibly 'for' the poor, but which, in fact, serve as systems of containment and control.

19

Rural Poverty in India and Development as a Policy Challenge

Poverty can be overcome, and that the poor can increase their income and production within an appropriate framework. Part of that framework is made up of a flow of resources and local-level institutional development, and there is considerable scope for improvement in both. However, the impact of investment and organisation is strictly determined by the nature of the policy environment. While project and programmes can bring some relief to the rural poor, substantial change needs a strong policy commitment. While the poor can overcome poverty, they will not be able to until this becomes a major focus of national policy and action. In the main, this sort of commitment has not been made in the past—at the expense of both the poor and overall development in many areas.

The current state of India is highly contradictory. On the one hand, there is proclamation of a new order; on the other, increasing value is given to sectional and short-term national and group interests. With an overt concern with the India's poor goes an equal weight given to concern with economic mechanisms and relations that pay little attention of poverty and foster more inequality. The dangers of this situation are real. The lack of concrete attention being given to change will mean greater economic polarisation. Greater polarisation among the better-off, and between the better-off and the poor—means instability and a lack of consensus, a lack of legitimacy.

Poverty is far-reaching, and ought to be curtailed. In a period in which resources everywhere appear restricted, this seems not to be an attractive proposition at the practical level. Welfare is every where giving way to production as an imperative, just as public expenditure is giving way to private accumulation. Poverty alleviation does not appear to be an idea whose time has come. The objections are great, but they are also misplaced. Poverty alleviation is not necessarily a drain upon accumulation, and it is not primarily a public activity. Poverty alleviation is primarily the activity of the poor themselves, and their progress necessarily involves productive expansion. If this potential for private expansion has not been realised, it is not because of the nature of the poor, it is because of the way in which national economic affairs have been organised. Economic policy has been oriented towards the better-off—not infrequently at the expense of the poor. Given the historic association between wealth and power, the definition of development in terms of the large and the wealthy is hardly surprising.

There is the possibility of associated growth involving both large-scale and small-scale production, the better-off and the poor. The realisation of this possibility might result from a new social compact. This social compact is not a commitment to social safety nets and welfare, both of which seem to presuppose that the poor are somehow necessarily out of the growth field. It is a commitment to abolishing artificial and onerous terms of exchange that discriminate against the poor, to investing resources where there are real opportunities for gain, irrespective of whether the economic agents concerned are rich or poor, and to creating the space for the poor to organise to pursue their social and economic interests.

There is a need for a new growth model consistent with new social realities. While the 1980s was a period of clearing away many of the obstacles to development, it was not a period in which there emerged a clear vision of what represented the positive basis for growth, beyond, this is, a general prescription of market-driven operations. The model must pass from admonition to positive prescription to fuel growth by integrating the poor in their rightful place in the production function. It must redefine the position of public expenditure in the development process, and seek to establish market structures which are both equitable and open to the participation of the economically weaker elements of the population. Most of all it must revalue the position and contribution of the poor and small-scale producers in the growth process, particularly in the agricultural sector, but not exclusively agriculture.

This means that the issue is not so much one of less government, but of government, both national and local, finding a new rationale for action, including, *inter alia*, creating conditions that will effectively unleash the productive potential of the rural poor.

Financial flows to the poorest Indians are not likely to undergo a very major expansion, especially through private channels. Development will rely very much on the mobilisation of their own resources, and many of these resources are in the hand of the poor, are, indeed, not only the human capital embodied in the poor but also their assets which, while small, individually are cumulatively important in India. The growth model for the 1990s will have to embrace that fact, and build upon it. The paradox of most development models is that they have emphasised the value of what Indians do not have, while devaluing what they have: capital intensity has been promoted in situations of scarcity of capital, at the expense of abundant labour and of low-cost methods of manifold increase of the productivity of assets of which the poor do dispose. In a not very indirect way, the creation of poverty has been subsidised. Poverty alleviation is neither a special topic nor a low-cost substitute for growth. It is neither more nor less 'social' than development in general. It is part of the formulation of any sustainable strategy of economic development. In the 1990s it may, and perhaps should, become the dominant issue—not as an alternative to the structural reorganisations of the 1980s, but as a means of filling a growth framework with substance.

20

Trade and Labour Standards

Using the Wrong Instruments for the Right Cause

A moral value is a shared concern of humanity; hence its enforcement should be a cooperative task implemented for the benefit of humankind. Would we qualify recent approaches to the issue of trade and labour standards as non-inquisitory but shared and cooperatives ones? The purpose of this brief is to shed some light on this question.

In fact, nobody, will deny any country the right to raise and fight for issues which are of moral concern for humanity, as they are supposed to benefit humankind. The issue of implementing and enforcing a core of labour standards one of these.

However, a problem remains: who has the negotiating power to raise and impose them? The key issue is that trade coercive attempts by some become inquisitorial as soon as they are backed by moral concerns which are supposed to be shared by all, while the same 'all' lack the negotiating power to be, in turn, coercive if they so wish. In other words, trade related coercion forcibly becomes 'inquisition' when moral concerns are introduced into the functioning of an international trading system characterised by large imbalances in the negotiating power of the participating countries. Only a few governments have the negotiating leverage and strength to develop what we may qualify as 'trade-related inquisitory practices".

The issue of trade and labour standards seems to have arisen when 'uniform competition' has been regarded as a threat to employment and economic growth in some industrial countries.

However, without attaining a certain degree of international agreement and coherence as to whether and under what conditions—a given competitive advantage is, or is not, related to social or other conditions, and whether or not it may be considered as 'unfair'. With protectionist views in mind, such an approach may only be interpreted as 'unbenign thinking' coming from 'unfair competitiveness seekers'.

If the motivation behind the introduction and further use of moral argumentation is to seek a justification for the possible use of trade measures as enforcement mechanisms to achieve certain goals. Particularly for harmonisation of labour standards, one may wonder why the labour standards issue has not been linked to North-North trade in the current debate on the considerable variation in labour standards among developed countries. The motivation may well be that in the post-Uruguay Round era, when tariffs have been reduced substantially and 'grey area measures' put under stricter control or even banned, we may be facing the possible revival of new forms of protectionism wearing 'blue', 'green' or 'multicolour' masks. On the contrary, if the motivation behind the introduction of such moral labour rights argumentation reflects a real commitment by the international community to enforce labour standards, a door may be open for embarking, in the future, on a series on international initiatives, not necessarily under the trade umbrella.

It should also be stressed that the linkage between trade and labour standards has been seriously misinterpreted. Most analysts remain blind to the two-way character of the link between trade and labour standards. On the one hand, trade liberalisation is to promote growth and development by promoting a more efficient allocation of resources and to ease the adoption and implementation of labour standards, as well as to promote job creation. On the other hand—and this is extremely important—raising labour standards—not keeping them low—should increasingly be seen as the real source of competitiveness and economic growth through, among others, increase in the quality of labour. There is a case for considering economic progress and the rise in labour standards as mutually reinforcing.

Turning to the low labour standards debate, much more empirical and analytical evidence is needed to assess the extent to which low labour standards and correlated to lower wages and labour costs. Although raising labour standards may not primarily be intended to maximise efficiency, it is becoming increasingly evident that efficiency and the future potential of the firm may not necessarily be maximised by keeping labour standards low. In this context, it is the development to human capital in LDCs which is a top priority, not because failing to respect labour standards in these economies threatens the welfare of the workers in the industrialised countries but, more simply, because it is the only strategy for enhancing the productivity of labour and ultimately increasing the people's standard of living. Thus, if raising labour standards and ensuring their effective implementation is important for economic progress, developed and developing countries, as well as workers and employers in each region, should adopt a cooperative, not confrontational, approach in order to deal with this urgent and pressing problem. For this very reason, adherence to trade sanctions would be a wrong approach. Trade is essential for enhancing workers' productivity because it ensures that a country's resources will be employed in the activities that it is best at. In turn, increased productivity is the key to development, higher labour standards and higher wages. Moreover, the issue of labour standards is of a moral nature; it has an undeniable development dimension which needs to be more clearly perceived but, as discussed, it is certainly not an issue to be dealt with through trade measures.

Labour standards should be dealt with in the WTO. The capacities of the ILO will prove invaluable for renewed multilateral effort to improve working conditions in developing countries. Its tripartite structure has proved to be the best suited to the tasks of conciliation and dialogue.

Improving the standards of living and labour standards for workers or eradicating child labour is what matters it is the right cause for humankind, a cause to fight for, through various approaches and by using all the mechanisms at our disposal in order to ensure its success. Thus, the issue is not one of trade and labour standards, but of labour standards and economic development, an issue of a human dignity and human rights nature. It is a universal issue, the solutions to which should be found by all nations, taking into account equity considerations. Each country should participate in the process, depending on its level of economic development. It is precisely because economic development, including trade, is positively correlated with the adoption and effective implementation of labour standards that solutions to low labour standards should not necessarily come from negative and coercive approaches. Solutions for universal problems must not only be efficiency-based but also equity-based. Therefore, the case is for cooperation rather than coercion and for applying positive instruments. As in the case of environmental issues, developing countries should be recipients of funds, technical cooperation and other similar forms of support when the implementation of labour standards involves an inequitable cost burden.

The initiative of 'grouping' a core of existing conventions into a new global convention on core labour standards of universal value may, in view of its new and distant qualitative nature, generate strong support from the international community for its implementation. The ILO was created to promote workers' right, so the initiative could be launched under its aegis, in direct collaboration with other intergovernmental organisations dealing with social, trade and development issues in an interrelated manner. The support to this or other similar approaches by the international community, and in particular by those developed countries that have recently shown a special and strong interest in the reinforcement and implementation of labour rights in developing countries, will be a clear sign of their degree of sincerity and their willingness to share the social concerns of universal value which seem to be of paramount interest to most of their citizens.

21

Challenging Traditional Economic Growth

Today, saving the planet is about redefining our economic development models. Striving towards the fulfillment of basic human rights is an integral part of environmental protection. Without a people-centered development strategy we will fail. Conflicting interests and lack of vision and courage are among the many reasons why its is so hard to meet needs in a world of plenty. We are faced with three major challenges in the 1990s.

- To curb population growth and poverty.
- To search for sustainable production and consumption patterns.
- To promote equity.

Population growth is often associated with poverty. But who causes the major strain on the environment? The 1.2 billion poorest people consume small amounts of the world's resources and contribute little to harmful emissions. They do not cause a heavy burden. The day-to-day struggle for survival of the poorest does, however, undermine their resources, and this causes deaths as population grows beyond the carrying capacity of nature. Here two key elements are essential: to tun from non-renewable to renewable resources, and to minimise use of resources through resource efficiency. We must single out the products and processes that must be phased out and those which may be allowed to expand. Right prices that include the ecological costs will be explored further, together with administrative measures. We are ready to examine to possibilities of using 'green tax' reforms to enhance employment and harness pollution and inefficient resources use. By shifting the burden of taxes from labour to environmentally harmful products and processes we might achieve a double benefit.

Transport, waste management, energy and land use are obvious areas that need to be affected by policy changes. Individuals must use their power as green-conscious citizens and shoppers—but in the end, producers and service providers hold the main key to practical action.

The market must be harnessed to meet people's needs both for present and future generations—starting by making economic policies play by the rules of nature. The World Trade Organisation (WTO) negotiations have provided us with instruments to regulate world trade.

Getting the Prices Right

Car emissions may be cut drastically, but the rapid increase of new cars nullifies the benefits. Even the most ardent technological optimist must admit that we need new priorities or cuts in some products and services. For example, we must improve public transport and resource-efficient cars—and reduce traffic.

Traditional economic growth models fall short of solving the problem of unemployment. Indeed, 'robots' and wasteful resource use replace people. There are great job-creating possibilities in environment-friendly produces and processes. Striving towards equity within and between nations, and within and between generations, is the major challenge of our time.

The fact that 20 per cent of the world's population consumes 80 per cent of the world's resources has too long been seen as mainly an ethical challenge. Ethics are not easily translated into politics, especially when confronted with economic and market realities. As equity gradually becomes a security issue—as it will, if we do not bridge the gaps within and between nations—it will climb to the top of the political agenda.

Many of the main conflict areas of today are battlefields of resource management. These will expand greatly if we do not turn conference statements of good intention into action. The 30-year old commitment of the rich countries to meet the target of 0.7 per cent of GNP in official Development Assistance remains unmet.

Two hundred years of Western-led development optimism reached its peak in the late 1980s. When the Berlin wall fall, the economic growth models of the rich countries had become the universal recipe. But as more and more people aspire to join the ranks of the middle classes, the resulting environmental stress calls for a halt, or a radical change of course.

The call for new patterns of production and consumption challenges our traditional concepts of economic growth and the focus on materialism in our culture. Neither the industrialised nor the poorer countries are strangers to radical process of changes, through the reasons for change are shifting. And we are truly facing challenging and conflict-provoking changes.

No nation by itself can solve the problems we face. Pollution knows no frontiers, but comes to us with the winds and waves. We have become more and more interdependent. If we are to attain sustainable development, we must commit ourselves through international agreements, through an international rule of law, through the development of financial mechanisms and through institutional agreements. We must develop means and tools to enhance collective security and mutual interests.

22
End of Controversy on Large Dams?

Was it worth the effort? The energy, the time, the money invested? Quite a number of people probably put this question to themselves on the 16th of November 2000 when Nelson Mandela launched the final report of the World Commission on Dams (WCD) in London. In an extraordinary process that lasted two and a half years, dam proponents, and opponents worked intensely together. Twelve commissioners had tried hard to come up with a consensus on the effects of large dams in the past, and with recommendations for future sustainable planning on water and energy issues. And surprisingly enough: the Commission succeeded. The cost of ten million dollars was financed by governments, international agencies, the private sector, NGOs and various foundations—this is also a novelty. Dam-affected people, non-governmental organisations, companies, consultants, politicians etc. contributed to the processes with their know-how and by giving support and additional resources to the Commission's work.

The establishment of the multi-stakeholder commission was the result of a growing and aggravating controversy about the social, ecological and-often enough also economic costs of large dams.

Global Review shows Faulty Planning Processes

The WCD Global Review of large dams proves that there were good reasons for massive resistance against large dams in the past. As the report says: "In too many cases an unacceptable price has been paid... especially in social and environmental terms, by people displaced, by communities downstream, by taxpayers and by the natural environment" while funders of large dams, political institutions, consultants and companies claimed in recent years that they had learned from their faults and improved their performance, the WCD highlights that, while policies and assessment procedures have been improved, it appears that business-as-usual too often continued to prevail:

- Even in the 1990s, impacts on downstream livelihoods were not adequately assessed or accounted for in the planning and design of large dams.
- Participation and transparency in planning processes for large dams was neither inclusive nor open, and while actual change in practice remains slow, even in the 1990s, there is increasing recognition of the importance of inclusive processes.
- Where opportunities for the participation of affected people are the undertaking of environmental and social impact assessment have been provided they often occur late in the process, are limited in scope and even in the 1990s their influence in project selection remains marginal.

Dams Hindered Human Development

The WCD states that "dams have made an important and significant contribution to human development, and the benefits derived from them have been considerable". A viewpoint that dam-affected people and NGOs hardly share, having in mind the experiences of the past. Medha Patkar, WCD Commissioner and activist in the struggle to save the Narmada river in India wrote in her comment to the Report: "Within the value framework the Commission propagates—equity, sustainability, transparency, accountability, participatory decision-making and efficiency—large dams have not helped attain, but rather hindered 'human development'.

The WCD also puts an end to the old viewpoint that the violation of human rights and the social costs that some have to pay can be justified by the benefits for the others. The idea that society as a whole would profit from so-called development that were benefiting from 'trickle down effect'. In fact this development model tends to aggravate social inequities and encourage environmental destruction leaving the rich better off, but the poor more marginalised and resentful. It is not a sustainable model.

It's Not Just About Dams

Although it is called the World Commission on Dams the issues before the Commission are much broader. The discussion about large dams is inevitably linked with the need to find solutions for supplying water and energy in the future. To do this in a sustainable way is one of the challenges of our time.

The WCD defined 5 crore values that are based on internationally accepted norms like the Universal Declaration of Human Rights to Development and the Rio Declaration on Environment and Development:

- Equity
- Efficiency
- Participatory decision-making and Accountability

These values are not really new and some of them have been agreed upon decades ago, but the Global Review of the WCD showed that 'in real life' we are still far from implementing them.

The rights and risks approach of the WCD must be mentioned as an important tool: while funders and dam-builders talk a lot about their (mostly) financial risks, risks of the dam-affected people were not a big issue in the past. The Commission makes an important distinction: while the former take a voluntary risk an have the possibility to decide on whether or not they want to take it, the latter take involuntary risks and so far had hardly any option in deciding on whether or not they are willing to incur them. Rights must not be violated in order to serve the needs of other people. Respecting human rights is the minimum basis for discussion and is not negotiable.

To get better results in the future the WCD defined seven strategic priorities for decision making:

- Gaining Public Acceptance
- Comprehensive Options Assessment
- Addressing Existing Dams
- Sustaining Rivers and Livelihoods
- Recognising Entitlements and Sharing Benefits
- Ensuring Compliance
- Sharing Rivers for Peace, Development and Security

According to the WCD there are several fundamental strategic points in the decision-making process. One point is right at the beginning of the planning stage: if the discussion about sustainable energy and resources management is carried out in a transparent, open and participatory process, further steps are much more likely to be accepted by all parties and will help prevent conflicts at later project stages. According to the WCD there are several fundamental strategic points in the decision making process. One point is right at the beginning of the planning stage: if the discussion about sustainable energy and resources management is carried out in a transparent, open and participatory process, further steps are much more likely to be accepted by all parties and will help prevent conflicts at later project stages.

The strategic priority 'Addressing existing dams' includes (among other policy principles) the identification and assessment of outstanding social issues associated with existing large dams. Considering that between 40 and 80 million people have been displaced by large dams (a lot more have been directly or indirectly affected) this is a difficult task. Financial institutions, development agencies and companies are a lot more interested in looking at the future than dealing with the complex problems of the past. But there is no way out. Dam-affected people of the past along with future dam-affected people are unlikely to accept new dams and believe in what is being promised while the legacy of the past is being forgotten. To solve these problems is a condition for further constructive discussions if not a mere moral obligation. How can those responsible for planning future dams think of gaining public acceptance if not by showing that they mean what they say?

The recommendations of the WCD are of fundamental importance, because they were agreed upon in a multi-stakeholder process. In other words, they were made by representative of industry as well as those from dam-affected people, by members coming from industrialised countries as well as those from developing countries. Within the Commission, it was possible to integrate the most diverse views and to come to a consensus.

No More Dams?

Although in their assessment the evidence would have allowed even stronger recommendations, NGOs and people's movements welcomed the report and asked for immediate implementation. Other stakeholders do not seem to be very enthusiastic about it. Quite a few representatives from industry and investors seem to fear that the implementation of the WCD recommendations would lead to an abrupt stop in dam building.

All appreciate that the WCD report vindicates many concerns raised by NGO campaigns. Given the role of financial institutions in funding large dams and in the WCD process, and based on the WCD report's recommendations, all has to call on all public financial institutions, including the World Bank, the regional development banks, the export credit agencies and bilateral aid agencies, to take the following actions:

- All public financial institutions should immediately and comprehensively adopt the recommendations of the World Commission on Dams, and should integrate them into their relevant policies, in particular those on water and energy development, environmental impact assessment, resettlement, and public participation. In particular, as recommended by the WCD, no project should proceed without the free, prior and informed consent of indigenous people, and without the demonstrable acceptance of all those who would be affected by the project.

- All public financial institutions should immediately establish independent transparent and participatory reviews of all their planned and ongoing dam projects. While such reviews are taking place, project preparation and construction should be halted. Such reviews should establish whether the respective dams comply, as a minimum, with the recommendations of the WCD. If they do not, projects should be modified accordingly or stopped altogether.

- All institutions which share in the responsibility for the unresolved negative impacts of dams should immediately initiate a process to establish and fund mechanisms to provide reparations to affected communities that have suffered social, cultural and economic harm as a result of dam projects.

- All public financial institutions should place a moratorium on funding the planning or construction of new dams until they can demonstrate that they have complied with the above measures.

23

A Breakthrough in the Evolution of Large Dams?

Back to the Negotiating Table

"The problem is not the dams. It is the hunger. It is the thirst. It is the darkness in a township". With these plain words, former South African President Nelson Mandela summed up the World Commission on Dams (WCD's) motives in a speech at the presentation praising its work. His position is similar to that of the many other representatives of the South who were present: he demands a right to development. But Ms. Medha Patkar, of India, a WCD Commission member and founder of the Struggle to Save the Narmada River (Narmada Bachao Andolan) anti-dam movement, takes a contrary view. "The problems of the dams are only a symptom of the larger failure of the unjust and destructive dominant development model," she says. We need to challenge "the forces that lead to the marginalisation of a majority through the imposition of unjust technologies like large dams".

Stagnation in Dam Building

The WCD is a unique experiment in reaching consensus. It began in April 1997 when with the support of the World Bank and the World Conversation Union (IUCN), 39 representatives of diverse interests met at a workshop in Gland, Switzerland. At this point the various positions of the participants from governments, the private sector, international financial institutions, civil society organisations and affected people were cast in stone. The Manibeli Declaration in June 1994 of 326 activist groups from 44 countries had called for an immediate moratorium on World Bank funded large dams until a comprehensive, independent review of all Bank funded projects had been conducted. International financial institutions were actually no longer able to fund further large dams in the face of public criticism. Enervated by steadily growing protests despite continual tightening of social and environmental standards, the institutions' representatives wearily likened the dispute to a football match in which somebody kept moving the goalposts. But one proposal to emerge from the meeting in Gland was for all parties to work together in establishing the World Commission on Dams.

The WCD began its work in May 1998 under the chairmanship of Prof. Kader Asmal, then South Africa's Minister of Water Affairs and Forestry. Its 12 members were chosen to reflect regional diversity, expertise and stakeholder perspectives. But the commission ran the risk of failure right from the start due to their confrontational attitudes. The members, who spent 2 years 6 months jointly organising hearings, consultations and case studies and analysing more than 100 existing large dams, could not be more disparate.

The Current Situation

A large dam is a dam with the height of 15m or more from the foundation. If dams are 5-15 metres high and have a reservoir volume of more than three million cubic metres, they are also classified as large dams. Using this definition, there are more than 45,000 large dams around the world, almost half of them in China. They were built in the 20th century to meet the constantly growing demand for water and electricity. On a the global scale, hydropower dams account for about 20 per cent of electricity generated, and in 24 countries, including Brazil, Democratic Republic of Congo, Zambia and Norway, hydropower covers more than 90 per cent of national electricity supply needs. Half the world's large dams were built solely or mainly for irrigation. Between 12 per cent and 16 per cent of world food production is based on dams, and the reservoirs they provide protection against floods.

Unfortunately, this impressive balance is counteracted by comparably significant problems. Construction of large dams is a major intervention in the ecosystem of rivers and the lives of many people. The WCD estimates that some 40-80 million people, mostly indigenous peoples, have been displaced by reservoirs worldwide and robbed of their livelihoods from fishing or farming. Serious conflicts are simmering between neighbouring countries because dams have turned off the water supply for downstream states.

The late Indian Prime Minister Jawaharlal Nehru once said: "Dams are India's new temples." Right up to the 1970s, large dams were seen as the synonym for development and economic progress. Dam-building reached its peak between 1970 and 1980, when an average of two to three new large dams per day were commissioned. But a considerable number of the dams analysed by the WCD have fallen short of their technical and economic objectives. Construction cost overruns averaged 56 per cent. Many dams have had negative ecological impacts, and the disadvantages for people living downstream were mostly not taken into account. The planning of dams did not examine sufficiently possible alternatives for meeting power and water needs. There were hardly any retrospective evaluations of dam projects.

A New Framework for Decision-Making

Despite this sobering stocktaking, the WCD arrives at an astonishingly simple finding: dams are primarily a means to an end. Their task is to improve the well-being of the people on a sustainable basis. This improvement should be economically acceptable, socially just and environmentally sound. If this goal can be achieved by a dam, its construction should be supported. Where alternative options offer a better solution they should be the preferred choice.

The Commission based its work on a set of five crore values for future decision-making: equity, efficiency, participatory decision-making, sustainability, and accountability. With regard to legal aspects and the extent of the potential risks for those involved, the WCD proposes development of an approach based on recognising rights and assessing risks. All risk-bearers should have a place at the negotiating table.

The WCD also recommends seven strategic priorities for decision-making: gaining public acceptance; comprehensive options assessment; reviewing existing dams; sustaining rivers and livelihoods; recognising entitlements and sharing benefits; ensuring compliance; and sharing rivers for peace, development and security. These priorities are reinforced by 23 practical criteria and guidelines which can be adopted, adapted and applied by all actors, involved in the dam controversy. For instance, the WCD suggests analysing points at issue together with the people affected by existing dams and developing joint proposals for solutions. People affected by new dam projects should be among their favoured beneficiaries, and their claims should be made legally binding.

The report offers a comprehensive compilation of knowledge, which previously was limited to individual case studies or a narrow specialist context, on the social, economic, technological and ecological problems and impacts of large dams. That makes the report a central reference which helps greatly in bringing objectivity into the debate. Provision of an analytical framework and strategic options is certainly an important step. But with regard to its task of developing internationally valid criteria and guidelines for the planning, design, appraisal, building operation, monitoring and shutdown of dams, the report remains very general. What will be decisive here will be to practice with the relevant actors the method and content of the suggested mediation process on the basis of specific cases.

Deeds Must Follow Words

The WCD's work must now be made useable for the private sector, civil society and development purpose. What is required is a discussion process involving all major actors. The objective of this process must be the development of practical and effective guidelines in addition to the current standards.

The WCD calls on bilateral development organisations and multilateral development banks to support only dam projects that have resulted from an open process of examining various options. The parties should observe the WCD guidelines. Measures to save water and power should be examined and, if applicable, be promoted.

Private sector companies should publish guidelines on corporate behaviour and acknowledge the WCD principles, criteria and guidelines. Further, the private sector should draw up and implement voluntary codes of conduct, management systems and certification procedures, such as the internationally recognised standard for environmental management (ISO 14001). The OECD's Anti-Corruption Agreement should be observed, and declarations of honesty incorporated in contracts. Business associations should develop processes to monitor compliance with the WCD guidelines.

NGOs should primarily check compliance with agreements and assist aggrieved parties to seek compensation. They should also assist in identifying relevant stakeholders for dam projects, using the rights and risks approach. Finally the NGOs should build up support networks and partnerships between them.

Importance of Information

But do these noble proposals provide the whole answer? The WCD process is based on the opportunities for personal development of every individual in an open society. But it is not enough to build on the negotiating abilities of the potentially affected alone because only specialists can anticipate the complex impacts of dams. Therefore participation presupposes that the mediation process contains a substantial informative component.

Relying solely on a mediation process is also not sufficient in providing for social impacts. There is no generally recognised method to determine the value of 'goods' in a subsistence economy. Without objective criteria, the moral demands on both sides are extremely high. Strategically-motivated behaviour will then not be prevented even if all participants agree readily that the subjective standard of living of people affected by a dam should be improved or at least maintained.

Mediation processes make sense only if agreements are observed. According to the WCD analyses, lack of compliance with agreements is the main cause of the negative social impacts of dams. In the case of dam projects co-financed by international donors, disbursements of funding installments could depend upon independent evaluations that confirmed compliance. Ensuring compliance is much more difficult in the case of projects financed by the private sector. Because there is no independent institution that could assume the role of arbitrator, it must be in the business world's own interests to act responsibly in ecological and social terms. To be credible, it must provide transparency and independent certifiers.

Due to the opposing interests involved, no-one should expect reaching consensus to be easy. But the example set by the WCD is not the only reason for hope. Taking a closer look at it, the model offers significant advantages for all participants. Partner countries and development organisations wish to continue to use the potential for development which dams will also offer in the future. The private sector will also continue to build and operate dams, and for that they need planning certainly. The advantages for NGOs and the people affected are also obvious.

24

Fighting for Equality on All Fronts

In the wake of unemployment, global competition and deregulation, more and more women are joining an unforgiving job market. Are they in a position to exercise force against the discrimination they experience, and can they impose equality of opportunity? To change things, women need to enter into combat on several fronts.

"For a long time, companies considered publicity to be a luxury and, in different times, the 'advertising and communications' budget was always the first to be slashed. Today, employers have become more aware that publicity has become a trump card in their strategy. Why can't a similar awareness become possible on the subject of women's employment?"

Financial problems and an evolution of mentality are the two core themes discussed in this paper on the Equality of Women in the world of work.

A Dual Observation

It is of a two-fold general observation: women are more increasingly joining the ranks of the active population: however, this trend is not matched by a parallel improvement in the quality of jobs to which they have access.

It is foreseen that women's rate of participation will be close to that of men by the year 2010. In developing countries, the rate of women's activity is only 31 per cent on average, but this figure does not take into account the very large female participation in the informal sector and in agriculture. Thus, for example, in India, the adoption of a more general definition of 'economic activity' pushed the participation of women from 13 to 88 per cent.

Women remained constrained in a relatively limited number of 'feminine' sectors and occupations which are generally less well-paid and are less prestigious. During the last decade, however, an upward trend has emerged and more women are acceding to management and administrative posts and to specialised and technical professions. Moreover, an increasing number of women are setting up their own businesses. It can be noted, nonetheless, that very few salaried women are able to reach the higher echelons of responsibility due to the well-known 'glass ceiling'.

Another other disturbing observations is the increase in part-time work, which is especially prevalent among women with young children; other types of a typical work include temporary and occasional jobs, homework and subcontracting. Part-time workers are often young women who are less educated and less qualified than the average, which makes them more vulnerable. In Africa, in Asia and in Latin America, women are being called upon more and more to find work in the informal sector.

Even though some progress has been made in the area of wages, women's salaries are still between one-half and 80 per cent of those earned by men. Women's work is underestimated in most of the societies, and their income does not match their contribution to the economy. The difference in wages cannot be attributed to conditions of work alone. In the United States, in 1994 a women in her twenties was likely to be earning 90 per cent of the rate of salary of her male counterpart.

Financial Problems

Financial problems and mentality issues emerged as two essential factors at every stage of the analysis of the causes of these persistent differences. The Fourm's participants' general consensus was that they should be tackled first of all.

Financial implications cannot be separated from the issue of women's employment, whether it is to justify its need or on the contrary to discourage it, or to explain the absence or lack of training of women who are available in the job market. Some examples are:

- In the countries in transition in Central and Eastern Europe companies underpressure to increase profits do not want to maintain social support services, which earlier had backed women's participation in the active population. These pressures are compelling women to leave the job market as the cost of child care increases.
- In developing countries, especially in Asia, Africa and Latin America, the worsening of poverty and the increase in the number of single-parent families are requiring women to turn towards income-generating activities, but the lack of training and difficult access to credit constitute a major handicap.
- In Thailand, one of the major causes of young village girls resorting to prostitution is the state of poverty of their families, who are unable to afford secondary schooling for them.

Prejudices and Stereotypes

Several examples can also be found in the persisting traditions and stereotypes which are an obstacle in the path of women's march to equality of opportunity in the world of work.

- The Nordic countries, in particular Sweden, have instituted a parental leave which enables either one of the parents to take care of the young children at home; but it can be noted that very few fathers avail themselves of this opportunity.

- The status of a profession falls as the number of women entering it increases; salary levels thus become relatively less competitive. This trend is particularly clear in the teaching professions and in some medical professions.

- Measures of positive action are becoming more and more general. They cannot be successful unless they tackle discrimination on all fronts, together with the fixed ideas that are prevalent on the subject of the sexes. In fact, solutions to the financial problems that women's work causes are themselves going through an evolution in mentalities.

In a highly competitive job market, opportunities available to women are conditioned by the comparative cost of women's labour, as it is perceived by the employer. By virtue of the legislation in force in the majority of countries, the obligations linked to maternity protection and family responsibilities tend to increase the direct costs of women workers; generally, employers bridge this gap by lowering the wages of women or limiting recruitment to childless women. This form of discrimination can also go as far as requiring medical certificate to guarantee sterility.

A Global Programme

To avoid such tendencies, efforts should be channelled toward two fronts. First, evaluating the relationship between a real cost-benefit (including the criterion of effective productivity) with a view toward eliminating the false idea that women workers are more expensive.

Secondly, making sure that in legislation, in practice and especially in the mentality of men and women all around the reproductive function and care of persons are recognised as social functions whose costs should be footed by society as a whole.

Recognising the universal nature of the problem and the various fronts where one would need to enter into combat, this programme should aim at changing the relationship of power between men and women. For this change to become permanent, it will be necessary to consolidate the ground gained as the process continues.

Remedies should be composed of measures touching upon, among other areas, legislation and its control, access to jobs, to training and to resources, the reconciling of professional activities with family responsibility, outreach measures to groups of underprivileged women, improvement of information and research, the participation of women in decision-making and the mobilisation of public opinion.

25

Crisis Prevention

Can Better Development Planning Lessen the Toll of Civil Emergencies and Natural Disasters?

Even a cursory scan of the world's headlines is depressing: armed conflicts are grinding on in Somalia, Afghanistan and in a growing number of other countries. And the effects of natural disasters are becoming more catastrophic each year. International relief aid, in response to such emergencies, has increased substantially. But how large can these sums of money realistically be expected to grow? With no end in sight to the need for relief, the good will of international donors is quickly giving way to disillusionment.

This leads us to a second question, which is, where does development fit in this grim scenario? For the development community to remain aloof from the issue of disasters and emergencies is not only politically short-sighted, it also ignores totally the causes and the effects of such phenomena.

Natural hazards such as hurricanes and earthquakes may be impossible to prevent. But they only become natural disasters if people are vulnerable. Why is it, for example, that an earthquake in Khilari, Maharashtra that registered 6.9 on the Richter scale killed up to 35,000 people, when an earthquake of almost the exact same magnitude in Los Angeles in 1994 claimed only 57 lives? By reducing poverty we can help increase the coping capacity of vulnerable populations. Therefore helping people lower such vulnerability is as much a development issue as the environment, or women's participation in development. Moreover, the repercussions of natural disasters go far beyond the immediate casualty list that so transfixes the media. Secondary and longer-term effects can be equally if not more devastating. And they must be taken into account by development practitioners.

It has been estimated, for example, that the damage to Mexico City's infrastructure form a massive 1985 earthquake amounted to US$ 3.6 billion. Yet over the subsequent five years, the negative ripple effect on the country's balance of payments resulted in a loss of $8.6 billion. Furthermore, reconstruction requirements forced Mexican authorities to revise their economic policies to meet an increased demand for public funding, credits and imports. The priorities for public expenditure were redirected to reconstruction projects, leaving many of the pre-disaster problems of the city and its people unattended.

In Bangladesh, floods in the recent past 2,000 people. But on closer examination we find that the toll was much more expensive than that: in each of these years the country's economic growth rate was halved by the delayed planting of rice and the destruction of seedbeds in the floods, further undermining the country's food security. All of these are consideration that go beyond relief, but they must be taken into account by development professionals.

Other emergencies may be more complex, but must be subjected to the same analysis. As the situations in Angola, Burundi, Somalia and the former Yugoslavia demonstrate, we know little about the dynamics of emergencies that arise from civil conflict. We do know, however that their cause usually lies in a lethal mix of poverty, poor governance and ethnic or religious rivalries exacerbated by profound social inequities. We are also learning that their resolution frequently requires the application of peacekeeping and political measures, combined with relief and development.

Among the most virulent effects of such complex emergencies is the massive displacement of people; women and children are the principal victims, constituting 70 per cent of the world's refugees.

These complex emergencies around the world could easily get worse before they get better. This being said, carefully designed development efforts—carried out as building blocks to national reconciliation in the fragile post-conflict stage will need to increase commensurately. The appropriateness and the sustainability of these development efforts will be one of the most important factors in determining whether peace itself becomes sustainable. For example, the absence of carefully tailored reintegration strategies for demobilised soldiers and their host communities would be an almost open invitation to resumed violence.

Yet we must also be conscious of the impact of aid and try harder to prevent the need for relief in the first place. An increasing body of evidence suggests, for example that emergency aid can sometimes be counter-productive in the longer term, increasing the vulnerability of populations and impeding recovery. Ironically, we find ourselves in situation today where it is far easier to obtain funds for maintaining refugees in their places of asylum than for helping them reintegrate into their own societies. In such cases, we may very well be helping to perpetuate the problem that we sought to relieve, as the presence of large numbers of refugees is sometimes itself a cause of conflict.

So how are we to proceed? And what exactly is the nature of the relief to development continuum that remains logical in the abstract but elusive in reality? The concept of a continuum does not imply a linear and absolutely progressive set of responses. On the contrary, it means that we are dealing with a set of processes rather than rigidly defined steps. It also means that development must be very much part of the disaster management process, and that the aim of the continuum must be to move from relief to rehabilitation and resume development at the earliest opportunity. However, this resumed development must include conscious measures to reduce the vulnerability that caused the disaster or the emergency in the first place.

In other words, we must give greater thought to prevention before we reach for the 'cure'—for humanitarian, political and financial reasons. (The Japanese insurance industry spends $ 200 million a year on disaster education alone). And as development practitioners, we must reconcile ourselves to the vastly more complicated environment in which we have to operate.

This means, for example that we will have to begin examining whether the economic policy 'medicine' often prescribed will reduce conflict or enhance it. We will have to ask ourselves if the reconstruction period following a civil conflict or natural disaster is the right time to advocate cuts in social spending, as has happened in certain countries in Africa and Latin America. Similarly, is it really in children's best interests to build a school in a seismic zone without first ensuring its structural stability? And does it really make sense to urge drought-prone countries to increase their reliance on cash crops, as has been done in some instances.

A story that never made headlines anywhere involves hundreds of the poorest people in Bangladesh, whose homes remained intact during the floods in 1988, when many others were simply washed away. These people were fortunate enough to have obtained credit through the Grameen Bank for construction materials as well as instruction in the building of flood-resistant homes. The Grameen revolving fund had received start-up capital from International Financial Agencies. Since that time the effort has been expanded, and more than 10,500 flood-resistant homes have been built in the last two years.

This is just one example of the kind of action we need more of—in fairly predictable and recurring circumstances such as the floods in Bangladesh, as well as in the more complex, man-made emergencies to which we must respond.

26

The Future of Work

The advent of an 'intangible' economy does not mean the end of work. But it does not mean the end of familiar routines and rhythms, of job security, of rigid hierarchies and career planning.

People are worried about the far-reaching transformation of the economy. Are we heading for 'the end of work'. Yes, we have reached the end of the road. We are no longer creating jobs in industry and automation is sure to reduce their number in the services sector. The quality of work is thus inexorably bound to decrease.

This thesis may be popular, but it is also mistaken and harmful. History shows that technological innovation has always created jobs on a large scale. In no way is the current trend leading to 'the end of work'. Just the opposite: the new economy containing huge pools of new jobs which can more than make up for the inevitable loss of traditional jobs.

Dematerialisation—the shift away from material products—is revolutionising all aspects of work-its nature, its organisation and its relationships with other activities. Its function is no longer just the manufacture of physical objects but the handling of data, images and symbols. The content of jobs is becoming more abstract. Skilled workers need to know a lot more about mathematics than their fathers or grandfathers did. Even milking cows and manufacturing require more and more calculation, evaluation and control.

Financial Markets That Never Sleep

The organisation as well as the product of work is also becoming increasingly intangible. The unity of time, space and action which characterized work in the industrial economy has disintegrated. Work is no longer a regular eight-hours-a-day, five-days-a-week routine. New rhythms have appeared—the hectic pace of financial markets which never sleep, the ups-and-downs of life in show business and the uncertainties of 'just-in-time' production where components are delivered a few moments before the final product is assembled.

The new jobs are quitting familiar workplace such as factories, offices and warehouses. Telework is increasing. Europe's teleworkers number rose to 10 million in the year 2000, from one million in 1994.

This upheaval of worktime and workspace is going hand in hand with a functional explosion. The range of skills and types of work is expanding all the times. In the United States, the number of job categories has risen from eighty in the 1940s to nearly 800 today. At the same time, trades are dying out faster and faster, especially in information technology where many jobs have a short life of only a few years. Jobs are becoming simultaneously more evanescent and more pervasive, more dissociated and more integrated. On the other hand, fragmentation in time and space seems to be more extensive than it was in the industrial economy. On the other, information technology is strengthening the links between different stages of work and creating an overall fluidity.

Disparities in Productivity

The new forms of work are non-linear. When handling information, knowledge and feelings, there is no direct relationship between the amount of efforts and the final result.

This makes for very wide disparities in productivity. In industry, the ratio of the performance of an average worker to that of a good one is no more than one to five. But in immaterial work, an excellent programmer can be a hundred times more productive than an average one.

Non-linear work means non-linear organisation. The notion of a rigid, formal hierarchy based on unchanging criteria no longer makes much sense. All that matters now is technical, scientific or artistic skills and the ability to establish a solid relationship with the customer. Functional hierarchy is replaced by 'brainpower'—authority gravitates to those who create and control the new stock of intangible assets: data, brand image, technological know-how and human capital.

The new techniques for managing human resources are individualising the assessment of performance. The two people doing the same job may have different salaries and different status. Automatic across-the-board pay rises are being dropped and replaced by bonuses linked to results. There are no sinecures in the new business enterprise, either for rank-and-file employees, supervisors or technicians—the supposed beneficiaries of the new knowledge economy.

Business leaders are no longer a protected species. The head of a big American firm is ten times more likely to be sacked for poor performance now than was the case twenty years ago. The notions of loyalty and of indissoluble links between a firm and its employees are losing their meaning.

The changing nature of work has led to a big increase in so-called non-typical jobs, including part-time, temporary and flexi-time work and short-term contracts. Almost all the jobs created in Europe between 1992 and 1996 were part-time. This trend worries many observers who see it as hidden under-employment or disguised unemployment. But they are overly pessimistic. The growth of non-typical jobs is the result of the convergence of several persistent developments.

Where the New Jobs Are?

The shrinking number of jobs in traditional sectors of the economy seems to be a general and irreversible trend. In rich countries as a whole, the share of industrial jobs fell from 28 per cent in 1970 to 18 per cent in 1994. Meanwhile, the share of the services sector grew steadily. Four major new sources of jobs can be identified:

Handling Information and Knowledge: Computer services, research and development, teaching and training account for 40 per cent of knowledge workers. These high-intensity knowledge activities comprised 43 per cent of all new jobs created in the United States between 1990 and 1995, but only 28 per cent of total jobs.

Information Technology: Here there is a shortage of personnel. Professional groups are sounding the alarm and calling on governments to help. In the European Union countries, the imbalance between supply and demand is such that half a million jobs are waiting to be filled.

The Health Sector: The growth of high-intensity knowledge services in this field is related to increased life expectancy and the ageing of the population, and the demand for physical and psychological well-being is also steadily increasing. The growth of expenditure on health is persistent and widespread. For the OECD countries as a whole, this spending grew from 3.9 per cent of GDP in 1960 to 7.2 per cent in 1980 and 8.4 per cent in 1992.

The Leisure Economy: This has triggered the expansion of cultural, sporting and leisure services. It ranges from amusement parks and rock concerts to cultural events such as opera and major art exhibitions. The products of the culture industries have become mass consumer items. Never before have people read so much, listened to so much classical music or visited so many museums. Information technology is also going to add to this vast range of consumer choice. In Southern California and New York, the entertainment and multimedia professions are among the main sources of new jobs.

In the labour market, the increase in non-physical jobs is one of the ways in which employers are responding to the pressures of competition and adapting to the global economy which functions seven days a week, twenty-four hours a day. To cope with the new situation, firms are having to figure out how they can use their workers more efficiently and flexibly.

The growth of non-traditional jobs is also due to changing demand. Consumers want to be able to buy a very wide range of goods and services at the drop of a hat, or amuse themselves any time, anywhere. To meet this demand, shops and places of entertainment have to be open late at night and on Sundays. Technology encourages this trend: the virtual economy of the Internet never sleeps.

The widening range of types of work also reflects long-term demographic trends, especially the greater number of women workers and longer life expectancy. Some see non-typical jobs as a necessary evil, while others, especially women with children, welcome the change.

The divide between traditional kinds of work and the new jobs is no longer watertight. People are increasingly switching back and forth between the two categories. In the course of a lifetime, a person may change from full-time to part-time work, from an office job to home office and from the security of a big firm to the adventure of entrepreneurship.

Changes in the nature of work are also breaking down the rigid frontiers which marked off the world of work. The traditionally distinct fields or work, education and leisure are now interwoven and coexist flexibly in a kind of triple helix of social life.

The emerging intangible and relational economy has a huge potential for growth because it is not bound by the constraints of material scarcity. However, the transition to the new economy is an open-ended process. The state has a key part to play in bringing it about. Governments can slow down the rate of change by making it more painful and more costly.

Obstacles to Change

Pessimistic scenarios are still plausible, such as that of an economy which generates few new jobs and is polarised between a small elite and the rest of the population who are marginalised and lie in precarious conditions. There is a big risk that this scenario will come to pass because current laws and regulations, as well as widespread pessimistic ideas about work, are powerful obstacles to change. Optimistic scenarios require a wholesale reform of institutional structures and profound changes in behaviour and attitudes. Such far-reaching changes often run into strong opposition from the social and political establishment and come up against the weight of psychological and social tradition. But the gamble of a new approach to work must be made if the transformation to the intangible economy is to succeed.

27

Population Growth and Income

Global economic output, the total of all goods, and services produced, grew from $5 trillion in 1950 to $29 trillion in 1998, expanding more than twice as fast as population. This increase of nearly six fold boosted incomes rather substantially for most of humanity. Growth of the world economy from 1990 to 1997 exceeded the growth during the 10,000 years from the beginning of agriculture until 1950.

Economic output per person climbed from just over @ 1,900 in 1950 to nearly @ 5,000 in 1997, a gain of 163 per cent. Although there is an enormous income gap between industrial and developing countries, the latter's economies are growing far more rapidly. Growth in industrial countries has slowed to scarcely 2 per cent a year during the 1990s, compared with nearly 6 per cent a year in developing nations.

The fastest-growing region in the world from 1990 to 1997 was Asia, which averaged nearly 8 per cent annually. This growth was led by China, whose economy has been increasing at nearly 10 per cent a year throughout much of this decade, making it the world's fastest-growing economy. Since 1980, China's economic output has doubled every eight years.

Incomes have risen most rapidly in developing countries where population growth has slowed the most, including, importantly, the countries of East Asia-South Korea, Taiwan, China, Thailand, Indonesia, and Malaysia, concentrating early on reducing birth rates helped to boost savings to invest in education, health care, and the infrastructure needed by a modern industrial society.

At the other end of the spectrum, African countries—largely ignoring family planning—have been overwhelmed by the sheer numbers of young people who need to be educated and employed. With population growth rates remaining at close to 3 per cent or more a year, most of any economic growth that occurred has been absorbed by the increasing population, leaving little to raise incomes.

The enormous growth during the 1990s, particularly in East Asia, is due to the huge increase in private capital flows into developing countries. Between 1990 and 1997, annual private capital flows increased from $42 billion to $256 billion, a gain of more than six fold. This substantial amount of money dwarfs traditional flows in public funds under international aid programmes.

Although incomes in much of the developing world are rising rapidly, they are not rising for everyone. The World Bank estimates that 1.3 billion of the world's people subsist on $1 a day or less. For this one fifth of humanity, trapped at a subhuman level of existence, there has not been any meaningful progress.

The sources of growth are changing. In earlier times, most of the growth was in agriculture. Since the advent of the Industrial Revolution, however, more and more of the growth has been concentrated in industry. Then beginning around mid-century, the services sector—insurance, banking, education—began to expand rapidly, accounting for most of the change in the industrial world. More recently, growth has been concentrated in the information sector as computerisation of the economy and telecommunications have grown at extraordinary rates.

The good news is that the global economy has been expanding at a near record pace during the 1990s, the bad news is that the economy, as now structured, is outgrowing the Earth's ecosystem. The result is excessive pressures on the natural systems and resources. As noted in the first section of this paper, from 1950 to 1997 the use of lumber more than doubled. That of paper increased six fold, the fish catch increased nearly five fold, grain consumption nearly tripled, fossil fuel buring nearly quadrupled, and air and water pollutants multiplied several fold, the unfortunate reality is that the economy continues to expand, but the ecosystem on which it depends does not, creating an increasingly stressed relationship.

If the economy were to expand only enough to cover population growth until 2050, it would need to grow from the $29 trillion of 1997 to $47 trillion. This, of course, would merely maintain current incomes, unacceptable though they are for much of humanity. If, on the other hand, the economy were to continue to expand at 3 per cent per year, global economic output would reach $138 trillion in the year 2050.

Even the first, more modest, growth projection would likely lead to a deterioration of the Earth's natural systems to the point where the economy itself would begin to decline. It is easy to foresee a scenario of continuing forest destruction, aquifer depletion, and ecosystem collapse that would lead to economic decline. If the world cannot simultaneously convert the economy to one that is environmentally sustainable—one that does not destroy its own support systems—and move to a lower population trajectory, economic decline will be hard to avoid.

28

For a Fair Sharing of Time

Women may have entered public life on a massive scale, but they are still on their own when it comes to running the household. A new balance must be struck if there is to be genuine democracy. At the dawn of the 21st century, states and the international community can no longer refute the fact that humanity is made up of two sexes, not just one. This discovery, a precious legacy of the century that just closed, has brought women's existence into the limelight. One of the great democratic challenges for societies over the next century will be to mature so that both sexes are able to live their lives on an equal footing, with all their differences, contrasting history and culture, but also with equal rights and responsibilities.

Women's rise to power and their participation in politics are the vital signs of a healthy democracy. If only this vision that emerged from the 1995 Beijing Women's Conference could spread worldwide! One can call it a radicalisation of democracy. When women take part in the public arena, contributing to the ongoing, shared effort to shape better ways of living together, a qualitative leap occurs. Their participation fills a gap which has until now prevented the emergence of a truly democratic culture.

Archaic Attitudes

But attitudes are not the only obstacle to women's ambitions. The structure of society and the way men and women run their daily lives are other stumbling blocks. The Inter-American Development Bank has had the good idea of giving the Institute for Cultural Action, and NGO in Rio de Janeiro, the task of setting up a pilot programme to train women for positions of political and social power. Participants include trade union and NGO leaders, key figures from the black and indigenous communities, company executives, civil servants and policymakers.

These women of different ages, educational backgrounds and ethnic origins are all aware of one fact: they are paying a very high price for a social contract that was negotiated when women were in a position of weakness, and agree that this has to change.

Re-Mapping the Division Between Public and Private Life

In Rio de Janeiro revealed that there is an urgent need to re-organise the use of time, to strike a new balance between responsibilities and to re-map the division between public and private life. Household tasks must be recognised as time consuming, socially and economically vital and a serious check on women's ambitions.

Women in positions of power must constantly prove that they can behave like men. They keep quiet about having to look after children, run a household and care for elderly parents. Bringing those issues out into the open would mean admitting 'flaws' that men do not have, for the simple reason that they delegate such work to their wives.

By drawing a veil of silence over their home life as if it were something illicit, women are allowing a basic fact to be hidden: the world of work relies on a domestic zone run by them. Women have changed, but the world of work has not and they are reaching the point of exhaustion. Filled with a deep sense of injustice, they are asking themselves: "where did I go wrong?"

Understanding that humanity is composed of two different but equal sexes has several implications. Society must redefine itself because women are turning up in public carrying children in their arms and breast-feeding them, and because they have their own awareness and language that come from life experiences which are different from those of men.

An Untenable Double Burden

Articulating issues affecting public and private life is complicated, but that does not mean the question is impossible of that the problems they raise should be brushed aside especially since the two worlds of public and private life are intertwined and mutually supportive. The balance between the two has now been upset. Women have entered public life on a massive scale, but the organisation of home life how time is used and who is responsible for what tasks is still the same, as if nothing had changed. And yet such a world, where women are expected to soldier on just as before, 'simply' adding to their lives experiences hitherto reserved to men, is called egalitarian.

The misunderstanding is fueled by an age-old tradition of dismissing the world of women, even by women themselves. Because society does not consider what they do in the home as having any major social significance, it fails to add this part of their lives to the other side of the equation.

This is why the massive migration of women from the home to the public arena is occurring without societies having to think seriously about how and by whom domestic work will be done in the future (and which women still do, but at what cost!) The double burden, resulting from an outdated social contract, is putting women under mounting pressure by speeding up their lives to an untenable pace. We are facing a social problem that society as a whole must solve and not, as many think, a problem that women must settle by working even harder.

As new areas of power open up to women, both sexes must take a fresh look at how they use time. Re-arranging it is a challenge to society's imagination. But has this necessarily sunk into the minds of decision-makers? I do not think so. This poses a major problem because it is a missing building block in the construction of our democracies.

The everyday work is proof of this. Women must put these issues on the political and economic agenda, thereby contributing to a more radical definition of democracy. Feminism's new demand for a different sharing of time also opens a debate that goes beyond the interests of women alone. In the final analysis, time and its constants define the limits of our own lives and the range of choices we make, in accordance with the meaning we give to our own existence.

The equality equation is increasingly complex. It is not enough to wipe out the last traces of discrimination in public life. A new definition of equality will emerge when both sexes start sharing responsibility in the private realm. Otherwise, the issue will be distorted and women will lose all chance of succeeding in public life.

29

Development: The People Know Best

Meetings of the World Bank and the World Trade Organisation has inspired high-minded protest and, on occasion, even vandalism. But this protest and vandalism may miss the point. It is hard to blame those who complain of bullying or blundering by the great institutions of global power. But the poor of the world, especially the poor of developing countries, deserve more than street demonstrations. The poor understand better than anybody the complicated details of their own poverty—the absence of health care, the lack of education, and all the sinister perils to their own safety and well-being. They know the failures of their governments, and of international institutions.

And that is the Point: It is the people of the poor countries who will have to apply new knowledge to design and achieve their own development. A country can only develop when its citizens have the freedom to address their own development problems. The obligation of the rich countries, is to give help where they can. And anyone who doesn't see a moral imperative to contribute to a fairer, more prosperous future is free to frame the obligation differently—as self-interest, for example. It will surely serve us better to invest in a peaceful and contended global community than to invite the strife and poverty of unanswered injustice and economic ruin.

Among our Relevant Conclusions: Powerful institutions of global finance and trade (not least, the World Bank and the World Trade Organisation) can be a source of real promise to poor countries. If governed right, they can help integrate developing economies into the enriching opportunities of global trade and investment. But such promise is often wasted because the very poverty of poor-country governments weakens their ability to negotiate the terms that would serve them best.

Communities in poor countries find themselves at a special disadvantage when it comes to bargaining with foreign investors. Investment can bring growth and spread wealth. It can also threaten human rights and social cohesion, or cultural integrity, and the fragile balance of ecosystems. Noble economist Amartya Sen has spoken powerfully about the intimate relation between development and choice, the subject of his thought-provoking book Development as Freedom. Development, Sen argues, "consists of the removal of various types of unfreedoms that leave people with little choice and little opportunity..." He defines freedom as "both the primary end and the principal means of development."

A precondition of this freedom is knowledge—knowledge of the hard facts and the hard science, on which real choices are constructed. Also it is knowledge of good governance—procedures of choice that are effective, responsive and democratic. For budgetary reasons, rich countries contribution to international development was severely cut in the 1990s. Now, along with others in the rich countries, they have to begin to reinvest in international development.

This means a new commitment to the improvement of lives, and to the future that the North must share with the South. It will be a reinvestment in peace, and in our own prosperity. This remains a matter of obligation, and of sensible self-interest.

30

An Agenda for Change

The World's growing population, combined with unsustainable production and consumption patterns, is putting increasing stress on air, land, water, energy, and other essential resources.

- Development strategies will have to deal with the combination of population growth ecosystem health, technology, and access to resources. Meeting the unmet need for family planning and reproductive health services should be part of national sustainable development strategies.
- The world needs to do a better job of forecasting the possible outcome of current human activities, including population trends, per capita resource use, and wealth distribution.

Protecting the Atmosphere

The atmosphere is under increasing pressure from green house gases that threaten to change the climate and from chemicals that reduce the ozone layer. Governments need to:

- Modernise existing power system to gain energy efficiency and develop new and renewable energy sources.

- Promote national energy efficiency and emission standards and develop efficient, cost-effective, and less polluting mass transit systems.

Combating Deforestation

Forests world wide are threatened by uncontrolled degradation and conversion to other uses because of increasing human pressure.

- There is an urgent need to conserve and plant forests in developed and developing countries to maintain or restore the ecological balance and to provide for human needs.

- Governments need to work with business scientists, local community groups, indigenous people, and the public to create long-term conservation and management policies for every forest region and watershed.

Sustainable Agriculture and Rural Development

Hunger is already a constant threat to over 800 million people, while the world's ability to continue meeting growing demand for food and other agricultural products over the long term is uncertain. Soil erosion, salinization, waterlogging, and loss of soil fertility are increasing in all countries.

Agriculture has to meet rising needs mainly by increasing productivity, because most of the world's best croplands are already in use. At the same time further encroachment on land that is only marginally suitable for cultivation must be avoided.

- Sustainable agriculture and rural development will require major adjustments in agricultural, environmental, and economic policies in all countries and at the international level.

Conservation of Biological Diversity

The loss of the world's biological diversity continues, mainly from habitat destruction, over-harvesting, pollution, of foreign plants and animals (known and exotics). This decline in biodiversity is largely caused by human activity and represents a serious threat to our development.

- Development national strategies to conserve and sustainably use biological diversity and to make these strategies part of overall national development efforts.
- Implement fair sharing of the benefits between providers and consumers of biological resources.
- Protect natural habitats. Promote the rehabilitation of damaged ecosystems.

Protecting and managing the Oceans

Oceans are under increasing environmental stress from pollution over-fishing, and degradation of coastlines and coral reefs. About 70 per cent of marine pollution comes from sources on land. Countries should commit themselves to control and reduce degradation of the marine environment. They should:

- Build and maintain sewage-treatment systems and avoid discharging sewage near shell fisheries, water intakes and bathing areas.
- Development land-use practices that reduce run-off of soil and wastes to rivers and thus to the seas. Use environmentally less harmful pesticides and fertilizers.
- Control and prevent coastal erosion and silting due to land uses such as unplanned construction.

Protecting and Managing Fresh Water

In many parts of the world there is widespread scarcity, gradual destruction, and increased pollution of freshwater resources. The causes include the inadequately treated sewage and industrial waste, loss of natural water catchment areas, deforestation and other chemicals into the water. The following approaches are key:

- The way to provide all people with potable water and basic sanitation is to adopt the approach "some for all rather than more for some". This approach can be achieved through low-cost services built and maintained at the community level.

- Nations need to identify and protect water resources and see that water is used on a sustainable basis. They need effective water pollution prevention and control programmes. There is a particular need for appropriate sanitation and waste-disposal technologies for low-income, high-density cities.

31

Do Men Matter?

New Horizons in Gender and Development

Why do men not feature more in gender and development policy? The shift in emphasis from Women in Development (WID) to Gender and Development (GAD), from enumerating and redressing women's disadvantages to analysing the social relationships between men and women, has not led to a recognition within policy of the need to understand the position of women and men. Is there a need for an explicit focus on men in GAD?

With a few notable exceptions, men are rarely explicitly mentioned in gender policy documents. Where men do appear, they are generally seen as obstacles to women's development; men must surrender their positions of dominance for women to become empowered. The superiority of women as hard working, reliable, trustworthy, socially responsible, caring and co-operative is often asserted, whilst men on the other hand are frequently portrayed as lazy, violent, promiscuous and irresponsible drunkards.

Why, then, focus on men? Emerging critiques of policy argue for special attention to be paid to men and masculinities in development as follows:

Gender is Relational

It concerns the relationships between men and women which are subject to negotiation in private and public spheres. To focus on women only is inadequate; a better understanding of men's perceptions and positions and the scope for changing these, is essential. Exploring 'masculinities' includes focusing on socially constructed 'ways of being a man rather than simply on their physical and sexual attributes, Biological essentialism is rejected in favour of an analysis of the social context within which gendered roles and relations are formed.

Equality and Social Justice

Gender concerns should not simply be viewed as instrumental in securing a more effective delivery of development. Instead, this critique recognises that men as well as women may be disadvantages by social and economic structures that they both have the right to live free from poverty and repression. Empowerment processes should also enable women and men to be liberated from the confines of gender stereotyped roles.

Gendered Vulnerabilities

Evident from several studies suggests that while women in general may face greater social and economic disadvantages, men are not always the winners and that generalising about their situation risks overlooking gender-specific inequities and vulnerabilities, such as the damaging health effects of certain 'masculine' labour roles or social practices.

Crisis of Masculinity

It is suggested that changes in the economy, social structures, and household composition are resulting in crises of masculinity in many parts of the world. The 'demasculinising' effects of poverty and of economic and social change may be eroding men's traditional roles as providers and limiting the availability of alternative, meaningful roles for men in families and communities. Men may consequently seek affirmation of their masculinity in other ways, through irresponsible sexual behaviour or domestic violence for example.

Strategic Gendered Partnerships

There is a strong argument that if gender equitable changes is to be achieved in households, communities and organisations, then surely men are needed as allies and partners? This links to concerns about the need to mainstream gender issues in development policy to ensure that they are not sidelined or under-funded as 'women's issues'.

Men and masculinities is a relatively new era in gender and development. Ideas concerning policy implications are in their infancy. How can research, policy, and training contribute to the debate and complete the shift from WID to GAD so that the situation of women and men is better understood? Suggestions include:

- investigating the changing roles, needs and identities of men over life courses;
- researching men's role in families, the reproduction of gender inequities through work, and men's specific health vulnerabilities;
- tracking and monitoring changes in gender relationships over time, in different cultural contexts, in association with programmes and policies;
- developing positive role models for men and boys influencing mass media image, establishing activities in schools, NGOs, religious and youth groups;
- ensuring that legal frameworks supports gender equity, through regulating working hours, parental leave provision, improved maintenance and inheritance law for example;
- improving gender training within development organisations to focus on gender and not women alone: for example by increasing the number of male gender trainers and improving gender analysis frameworks.

32

Social Development: The Way Forward

The idea of development is seductive; it is also elusive. It promises a lot to everyone, but it has failed to deliver to those in greatest need. In 1944 development and economic growth were largely synonymous, but by the 1950s, when it became clear that this model was not helping the poor, a focus on social development evolved. Its advocates argued that economic growth as development should be pursued, but complemented with social development programmes for those who were 'excluded'. This approach did not fare much better, and the idea of socio-economic development, in which social development principles were to be mainstreamed in the economic growth process, was born.

Social development is commonly used to include the policies and programmes designed to combat poverty, unemployment, crime, social exclusion, ill health and illiteracy—all noble causes. But noble intentions do not easily produce the desired results; they sometimes produce the opposite. Most social development programmes, in both developed and developing countries, run the risk of fostering the victim mentality, creating dependency and deepening disempowerment, although they seek the reverse.

The 1995 Social Summit in Copenhagen, which addressed the themes of poverty, unemployment and social exclusion, was a significant milestone in the history of development. Apart from its direct outcomes in the form of commitments and an action plan adopted by well over 100 heads of states, the summit raised the political profile of social development. But five years later, while several developing countries managed real improvements in their social development indicators, the problems identified at Copenhagen are still with us and many have worsened. The main reasons for this are the usual one—lack of new and additional resources and lack of political will.

The results of the Social Summit review will be presented at the Special Session of the United Nations General Assembly in Geneva shortly. Hopefully, the Special Session will generate not only innovative solutions, but also the political will to carry them out. The General Assembly three simple and somewhat basic recommendations should be kept in mind:

- Reiterate poverty eradication as the top priority of the international and national development agenda.
- Recommended an operationally enhanced human development strategy as the practical framework for development cooperation for poverty eradication.
- Encourage development agencies and governments to use their existing sectoral mandates as entry points in a synergistic framework provided by the operationally enhanced human development framework, which could also be called a sustainable livelihood approach.

All of the above are politically and operationally feasible. The implication of the first is to focus on the single theme of poverty eradication for action over the next five years. Social exclusion could be addressed in the strategy for poverty reduction, and employment should be seen as one of the entry points for action in the strategic action framework for poverty eradication. This provides a clear agenda around which political will, resources and action can be mobilised.

The second and third proposals addressed the weaknesses of the welfare and/or growth and trickle down approaches to poverty eradication in current vogue. Such a social agenda creates a no-win situation, in the sense that even when it succeeds in squeezing out some reprieve for workers, the poor and the disadvantaged, it produces more victims waiting to be saved and so fosters a pervasive disempowerment process. Further, and more importantly, the rationale places the economy before people.

The human development approach offers a powerful and viable alternative by fundamentally reversing the premise on which development planning proceeds—to put the economy at the service of the people rather than the reverse. The question then is how to address the social development agenda through an enhanced human development approach?

At the operational level, the following would greatly enhance the human development approach to poverty eradication:

- Begin by focusing on what people have (the assets approach), not what they need by defining assets broadly to include human, social, national and physical capital.
- Understand people's adaptive strategies to shocks and stresses and seek to further develop and release their creativity by appropriate policy, governance, technology and investment shifts and inputs.
- Mainstream the environment by giving natural capital the same level of importance as human, social and physical capital in the programme design framework.
- Mainstream gender by paying attention to different patterns of asset ownership by men and women and their different adaptive strategies.

On an optimistic note, the evolution of development practice has more often than not been characterised by a willingness to learn from past mistakes and to move forward with new and innovative paradigms. This spirit must continue if the dream of a poverty-free world is to be realised.

33

Gender-Based Violence

Around the world atleast one woman in every three has been beaten, coerced into sex, or otherwise in her life time. Most often the abuser is a member of her own family. Increasingly, gender based violence is recognised as a major public health concern and a violation of human rights.

The effects of violence can be devastating to a women's reproductive health as well as to other aspects of her physical and mental well-being. In addition to causing injury, violence increases women's long-term risk of a number of other health problems, including chronic pain, physical disability, drug and alcohol abuse, and depression. Women with a history of physical or sexual abuse are also at increased risk for unintended pregnancy, sexually transmitted infections, and adverse pregnancy outcomes. Yet victims of violence who seek care from health professionals often have needs that provides do not recognise, do not risk ask about, and do not know how to address.

What is Gender-Based Violence

Violence against women and girls includes physical, sexual, psychological and economic abuse. It is often known as 'gender-based' violence because it evolved in part from women's subordinate status in society. Many cultures have beliefs, norms, and social institutions that legitimise and therefore perpetuate violence against women. The same acts that would be punished if directed at an employer, a neighbour, or an acquaintance often go unchallenged when men direct them at women, especially within the family.

Two of the most common forms of violence against women are abuse by intimate male partners and coerced sex, whether it takes place in childhood, adolescence, or adulthood. Intimate partner abuse—also known as domestic violence, wife-beating, and battering—is almost always accompanied by psychological abuse and in one-quarter to one-half of cases by forced sex as well. The majority of women who are abused by their partners are abused many times. In fact, atmosphere of terror often permeates abusive relationships.

How Health Care Providers can Help

Health care providers can do much to help their clients who are victims of gender-based violence. Yet providers often miss opportunities to help by being unaware, indifferent, or judgemental. With training and support from health care systems, providers can do more to respond to the physical, emotional, and security needs of abused women and girls.

First, health care providers can learn how to ask women about violence in ways that their clients find helpful. They can give women empathy and support. They can provide medical treatment, offer counselling, document injuries and refer their clients to legal assistance and support services.

Family planning and other reproductive health care providers have a particular responsibility to help because:

- Abuse has a major—although little recognised—impact on women's reproductive health and sexual well-being.
- Providers cannot do their jobs well unless they understand how violence and powerlessness affect women's reproductive health and decision-making ability.

- Reproductive health care providers are strategically placed to help identify victims of violence and connect them with other community support services.

Providers can reassure women that violence is unacceptable and that no woman deserves to be beaten, sexually; abused, or made to suffer emotionally.

Societal Responses

Health workers alone transform the cultural, social, and legal environment that gives rise to and condones widespread violence against women. Ending physical and sexual violence requires long-term commitment and strategies involving all parts of society. Many governments have committed themselves to overcoming violence against women by passing and enforcing laws that ensure women's legal rights and punish abusers. In addition, community-based strategies can focus on empowering women, reaching out to men, and changing the beliefs and attitudes that permit abusive behaviour. Only when women gain their place as equal members of society will violence against women no longer be an invisible norm out, but, instead, a shocking aberration.

Bibliography

Allchin, B. and Allchin, R.,—*Civilization: India and The British of Indian Pakistan Before 500 B.C.*, London, 1968.

All India Economic Conference, *Economic life of Hyderabad*, Government Central Press, Hyderabad, 1937.

Andhra Pradesh, Government of, *Hand Book of Statistics*, Andhra Pradesh, 1993-94, p. 235.

Andhra Pradesh, *Government of Economic and Statistical Bulletin, Vol. XXXVII, No. 11, July-December, 1992*, Directorate of Economics and Statistics of Hyderabad, p. 10.

Andhra Pradesh, Government of, *Hand Book of Statistics*—Andhra Pradesh, 1993-94, Directorate of Economics and Statistics, Hyderabad, 1995, p. 7.

Andhra Pradesh, Government of, *Statistical Abstract of Andhra Pradesh, 1992*, Directorate of Economics and Statistics, Hyderabad, 1994, p. 111.

Andhra Pradesh, *Government of Statistical Abstract of Andhra Pradesh, 1992*, Directorate of Economics and Statistics, Hyderabad, 1994, p. 111.

Agro-Economic Research Centre, *"Rice in Andhra Pradesh—A Study on Inter State Variations, Kharif, 1978, Part—I, Report"*, The Author, Andhra University, Waltair, September, 1982, pp. 15-34 and 59-69.

Apinantara, Adul., *"Cooperation and Water Conflicts Among Water Users in North Eastern Thailand Tank Irrigation"*, ADC, Workshop, Bangkok, Thailand, 1981 (Mimeo).

Appadorai, A. *Economic Research Centre in Southern India (1000-1500) A.D.*, University of Madras, 1936.

Arputhraj, C., *"Problems and Prospects of Tank Irrigation in Tamil Nadu"*, Workshop on Modernisation of Tank Irrigation, Problems and Issues, Centre for Water Resources, Madras, 1982 (Mimeo).

Chambers, Robert, *"Men and Water: The Organisation and Operation"* in B.H. Farmer (ed), *Green Revolution*, Macmillan, London, 1977.

Cgrabheevyky, P., *Tank Irrigation and Agricultural Development*. Kanishka Publishing House, New Delhi, (India), 1992.

Coward, Sr.E. Walter, *Irrigation and Agricultural Development in Asia*, Cornell University Press, U.S.A., 1980.

Das Gupta, Kalyan Kumar, *et. al.* "Problems of Management of Tank Irrigation", *Impact of Tank Irrigation: A Case Study of Tumkur District*, Himalaya Publishing House, New Delhi, 1978.

Dean. D.J. and Fray. T.L., "Discriminant Analysis of Loans for Cash Grain Farmers", *Agricultural Economic Review*, Vol. 36 (Annual) (April 1976).

Doherty, Victor S., *"A Cross Cultural Analysis of Tank Irrigation", Workshop on Modernisation of Tank Irrigation: Problems and Issues"*, Centre for Water Resources, Madras, India, 1982.

Department of Agricultural Engineering, *"Development and Optimisation in the use of Irrigation Water under Ex-Zamin Tank in Ramanathapuram District"*, Preliminary Report, Government of Tamil Nadu, Madras, India, 1982.

Elumalai, G., *"Modernisation of Tank Irrigation Systems—Farmer's Views" Workshop on Modernisation of Tank Irrigation: Problems and Issues*, Centre for Water Resources, Madras, 1982 (Mimeo).

Evaluation and Applied Research Department, Government of Tamil Nadu, *"Evaluation of Minor Irrigation Schemes"*, Second Regional Workshop on Evaluation, Madras, India, 1979.

George. P.T.., Namasivayam. D. and Ramachandraiah. G., *"Application of Discriminant Function in the Farmers' Repayment Performance: A Study in Chingleput District, Tamil Nadu", Journal of Rural Development*, Vol. 3. No. 3 (May 1994).

George W. Snedecor and William G. Cochran, *Statistical Methods*, New Delhi, Oxford and IBH Publishing Co., (Sixth Edition), 1967.

Gupta S.C., *Development Banking for Rural Development*, New Delhi, Deep and Deep Publications, 1987.

Hand Book of Statistics: Ananatapur District, 1991-92 and 1992-93, Chief Planning Office, Anantapur, n.d. p. IV.

Harris, D.G., *Irrigation in India*, Oxford University Press, London, 1923.

Hayami, Y., Bennagem, E. and Barker, R., *"Price Incentive versus Irrigation Investment to Achieve Food Self-Sufficiency in Philippines", American Journal of Agricultural Economic*, Vol. 59, No. 4, 1977, p. 717-721.

India, Government of., *Eighth Five Year Plan, 1992-97*, Vol. II, 1992, p. 56.

India, Government of, "Report on Minor Irrigation Works in the State of Madras" Committee on Plan Projects, 1959.

India, Government of, *Census of India 1991—Final Population Totals*, Vol. II, Series 1, Paper 1, 1992, Ministry of Home Affairs, Government of India, New Delhi, p. 115.

India, Government of, Programme Evaluation Organisation, *A Study of the Problems of Minor Irrigation*, Planning Commission Publication, No. 140, 1961, pp. 7-103.

Indian Agricultural Statistics, for the Years 1891-92 to 1947-48.

Janakarajan, S. *"In Search of Tanks: Some Hidden Facts", Economic and Political Weekly*, Vol. XXVII, No. 26, June 26, 1993, pp. A-53—A-60.

Jayabalan, B.A., *"Modernisation of Tank Irrigation in Tamil Nadu"*, Workshop on Modernisation of Tank Irrigation Problems and Issues, Centre for Water Resources, Madras, 1980.

Jha, U.M., *Importance of Irrigation in an Ararian Economy, Irrigation and Agricultural Development*, Deep and Deep, New Delhi, 1984.

Lakadawala, D.T., *"Growth, Employment and Poverty"*, Presidential Address, All India Labour Economics Conference, Tirupati, December, 1977.

Madras Institute of Development Studies, *"Tank Irrigation in Tamil Nadu—Some Macro and Micro Perspectives"*, (Report—Mimeo), 1983.

Mukundan, T.M., *"The ERY System of South India"*, PPST Bulletin, Madras, September, 1988.

Namerta, *"Growth and Spatial Pattern of Market Towns in Rayalaseema Region of Andhra Pradesh"* Unpublished M.Phil Thesis, Submitted to Jawaharlal Nehru University (Centre for Development Studies), New Delhi, 1989.

Narayana Rao, J.S., *"Irrigation and Planning in Andhra Pradesh"*, Conference Papers of Andhra Pradesh Economic Association, Sixth Annual Conference, 23-24 January, 1988, pp. 145-150.

National Institute of Rural Development, *Rural Development Statistics: 1994*.

Narain, Dharan, and Roy B. Shyamal, *"Impact of Irrigation on Labour Availability and Multiple Cropping"*, International Food Policy Research Institute, Research Report, 2-0, 1980, pp. 7-8 and 26.

"Need for Restoration of Tanks:, The Hindu, August 8th, 1991, p. 3.

Narain, *et. al.* *"An Approach to Study of Irrigation—A Case Study of Kanyakumari District; Economic and Political Weekly*, Vol. XVII, No. 39, September 25, 1982, p. 485.

Palani Swamy, K., *"Irrigation Tank Rehabilitation"*, *The New Irrigation Era*, Vol. XIX, No. 3, 1981, pp. 36-37.

Palaniswamy, K. and Easter, K.W., *"The Tanks of South India: A Potential for Future Expansion in Irrigation)"*, Economic Report, Department of Agriculture and Applied Economics, University of Minnisote, No. 83.4, 1983.

Rao. G.N. and Rajasekhar, D., *"Tank Irrigation in Andhra Pradesh: A Case Study"* Conference Papers of Andhra Pradesh Economic Association, Second Annual Conference, January, 1985, pp. 57-70.

Rao, V.M., *"Linking Irrigation with Development—Some Policy Issues"*, Economic and Political Weekly, Vol. XII, No. 24 1978, pp. 993-97.

Rajasekhar, D., *Land Transfer and Family Partitioning* Oxford and IBH Publishing Company, New Delhi and Centre for Development Studies, Trivandrum, 1988.

Rao, N.V.N., and Ram Reddy, R., *"Minor Irrigation and Tribal Development—An Empirical Study"*, *Kurukshetra*, Vol. XXXIV, No. 2, November 1995, pp. 31-33.

Ramaswamy, V. *et. al.* *"Damasi: A Concept of Equity and Productivity in Irrigation"*, *Wamana*, Vol. V, No. 3, July, 1985, pp. 1 and 15-22.

Ramanathan, *"Tank Irrigation in Tamil Nadu"*, unpublished M.Phil Thesis, The Jawaharlal Nehru University, 1985, pp. 70-137.

Reddy, Narasimha, D., *"A Note on the Decline of Tank Irrigation"*, Paper Presented At Lokayan Workshop on Tank Irrigation, Bangalore, July, 1988.

Rao, V.M., *"Linking Irrigation with Development—Some Policy Issues"*, Economic and Political Weekly, Vol. XII, No. 24, July 17, 1978, pp. 993-997.

Rami Reddy. S., *"Factors Discriminating Defaulters from Non-defaulters in Primary Credit Cooperatives"*, Indian Cooperative Review, Vol. 14. No. 1 (October 1976).

Satis, S. and Sundar, A., *People's Participation and Irrigation Management: Experiences, Issues and Options*, Commonwealth Publishers, New Delhi, 1990.

Sakthivadivel, R., *et. al.*, *"A Pilot Project Study of Modernization of Tank Irrigation: Problems and Issues"*, Centre for Water Resources, Madras, 1982. (Mimeo).

Sen Gupta, Nirmal., *Managing/Common Property: Irrigation in India and the Philippines*, Sage Publications, New Delhi, 1991.

Sen Gupta, Nirmal, *"Irrigation: Traditional Vs. Modern"*, Working Paper No. 55, Madras Institute of Development Studies, Madras, April 1985, p. 5 (Mimeo).

Sen Gupta Nirmal., *Tank Irrigation in Gangetic Bihar*, A.N.S. Institute of Social Studies, Patna, Bihar, 1982.

Sivanappan, R.K., *"Water Management in Tank Irrigation in Tamil Nadu"*, Workshop on Modernisation of Tank Irrigation: Problems and Issues, Centre for Water Resources, Madras, 1982 (Mimeo).

Sivamohan, M.V.K., and Christopher A. Scott, (Ed), *India: Irrigation Management Partnerships*, Booklinks Corporation, Hyderabad, 1994.

SPSS Inc., SPSS/PC Release 1, 1 Update the Author, U.S.A., 1984, pp. B. 202-204.

Sundar, A., and Rao, P.S., *"Farmers' Participation in Tank Irrigation in Karnataka"*, Workshop on Modernisation of Tank Irrigation" Problems and Issues, Centre for Water Resources, Madras, India, 1982.

Srinivasan, T.M., *Irrigation and Water Supply: South India 200 B.C, 1600 A.D.*, New Era Publications, Madras, 1991.

Subbalkshmi, V., *"Incorporation of India and Indigenous Irrigation Institutions: The Case of Dasabandam in Rayalaseema"*, Conference Papers of Andhra Pradesh Economic Association, Sixth Annual Conference, January, 1988, pp. 114-128.

Smith R. Baird, *Irrigation in Southern India*, Elder and Co., London, 18567, Ch. 6.

Tubpin, Y., Easter, K.W; Welsch, D., *"Tank Irrigation in North-Eastern Thailand, The Returns and Their Distribution"*, Economic Report, Department of Agricultural and Applied Economics, University of Minnesota, No. Er, 82-6; 1982, p. 66.

Uma Shankari, *"Tanks: Major Problems in Minor Irrigation"*, *Economic and Political Weekly*, Vol. XXVI, No. 39, September 28, 1991, pp. A115-A125.

USAID, *"Thailand North-East Small Scale Irrigation"*, Washington, D.C., 1980.

Vasudeva Rao, D. *Rural Development Through Irrigation*, New Delhi, Ashish Publishing House, 1987.

Venkatram, B.R., *"Administrative Feasibility of Tank Irrigation Authority"*, Economics Programme, Consultancy Report, ICRISAT, Hyderabad, Andhra Pradesh, 1980, pp. 1-4.

Von Oppen, M. and Subba Rao, K.V., *"Tank Irrigation in Semi-Arid Tropical India, Part-I: Historical Development and Spatial Distribution"*, ICRISAT, Economics Programme Progress Report, 5, Andhra Pradesh, India, 1980, p. 1.

Von Oppen, M. and Subba Rao K.V., *"Tank Irrigation in Semi-Arid Tropical India, Parts, I, II, and III"*, Progress Report, ICRISAT, Hyderabad, 1980.

Von Oppen, M. and Subba Rao, K.V., *"History and Economics of Tank Irrigation in Semi-Ouid Tropical India"* Symposium on Rain Water and Dry Land Agriculture, Indian National Science Academy, New Delhi, 1982, pp. 89-93.

Von Oppen, M., *"Tank Irrigation in Southern India: Adopting a Traditional Technology to Modern Socio-Economic Conditions"*, Proceedings of the Consultants' Workshop on State of the Art and Management Alternatives for Optimising the Productivity of SAT Alfisoils and Related Soils, ICRISAT, Patacheru, Hyderabad, Andhra Pradesh, India, 1987, pp. 89-93.

Wijayaratna, C.M., *"Uneven Distribution of Water: Causes, Consequences and Implications for System Management"*, Workshop on Water Management, Agrarian Research and Training Institute, Colombo, Sri Lanka, 1982, (Mimeo).

Yazdani, G. (Ed), *The Early History of Deccan*, Oxford University Press, London, Parts-VI, 1960.

Index